A WHITE FACE PAINTED BROWN

Kellye,

May the love of
Christ be with
you always.

Kathleen Bishop

A WHITE FACE PAINTED BROWN

by KATHLEEN BISHOP

PALLAS ATHENA
PRESS

This is a true story but the names and identities of some characters have been changed to protect their privacy.

Printed by Delta Lithograph Co., Valencia, CA.

Edited, designed and typeset by Delta Electronic Publishing, Fremont, CA.

Published by
Pallas Athena Press
P.O. Box 326
Fairfield, CA. 94533-0032

Library of Congress Catalog number: 93-084258

ISBN: 0-9636217-1-8

Printed in the U.S.A.

This book is dedicated
to all ghetto children
whose lives are a testimony
to their courage and their love

Acknowledgments

I would like to extend my appreciation to the following people:

To my husband Al, for his support, encouragement and love — without it there would never have been a book.

To my two children, Michelle and AJ, who have deeply touched my life with their laughter and their love.

To my mother, for instilling in me her love of learning.

To my godparents Gilbert and Maria, and their children Christian, Nicky and Marisa Parisi, for always making me feel like a member of their family and a part of their lives.

To my sister-in-law Sylvia and her children Marisa, Tony, Sylvia and Raymond Medina, for the special friendship we have shared for so many years.

To my sister Pat, for the contribution of her personal story.

To my brothers Mike and Billy, my brother-in-law Steve and my sister Carrie, for all the special times we have shared together.

To a great editor, Joanne Shwed, for the long hours of work and superb job she performed on my manuscript.

Contents

iii

Foreword

I would like to address this book to several different groups ... teachers ... doctors ... social workers ... policemen ... and all those who have a sincere desire to understand and take an active part in changing the destiny of ghetto children in America.

I bring an intimate knowledge of ghetto children that can only be gained through experience. For that reason, I think this book would be very effective in the training of any professionals who work with ghetto children:

Teachers have the greatest opportunity to change the destiny of ghetto children. However, this opportunity is often lost because teachers, who have rarely experienced the ghetto themselves, cannot see the world *from* a ghetto. This book has the power to change that: it takes a long, hard look at the internal environment that shapes a ghetto child from within.

Doctors have a tremendous opportunity to protect ghetto children from premature death. This opportunity is often lost on doctors who have seldomly been required to develop a perception

— much less a sensitivity — towards their small patients. This book has the power to change that: it illustrates the negative and positive dimensions of the medical profession in this country and its far-reaching impact on the lives of ghetto children.

Social workers have the unique opportunity to examine the intimate details of a child's life . . . a mother's life . . . and the family as a unit. That opportunity is often lost on social workers who frequently look the other way from physical abuse, parental substance abuse, sexual abuse, and all the circumstances that differentiate a ghetto from the world outside. This book has the power to change that: it requires social workers to examine why the people they serve so often see them as the blind leading the blind.

Policemen have a powerful opportunity to curb violence in ghettos by becoming an instrument of peace themselves. That opportunity is often lost on the unwarranted beatings, verbal insults and complete lack of respect customarily shown towards ghetto people. This book has the power to change that: it demonstrates the internal damage policemen inflict on ghetto people and its long-term impact on the development of ghetto children.

The haunting memories of my childhood will never let me forget all the children that continue to be trapped there. Their prison is the psychological boundaries created by their experiences. Their only hope is if we, as a nation, can develop a collective perception based on the reality of their lives, and offer the opportunity to develop the tools within themselves to escape the ghetto.

Introduction

On my way home from school, my eyes always scanned the familiar spray-painted messages sprawled out across the brick walls of Aliso Village, a housing project bordering East Los Angeles. A fresh, new one strikingly stood out from among the rest — a famous Mexican saying that I heard before but never saw in print. I felt the emotion of the sweeping strokes that formed the red letters splashed across the wall: *I would rather die on my feet than live on my knees.* I was struck by the sudden realization that the spirit of an entire race of people could be contained inside of one sentence. It was on that day that I learned to understand why the pen is mightier than the sword.

I grew up among a fiercely proud people who taught me to fight with my spirit, unafraid of death. The greater death was not in losing one's life but in losing one's self-respect.

The clenched jaw of the black faces that surrounded my childhood and the defiant fists raised up high in the air against the enemy, to whom I was the physical embodiment, would create a situation where the spiritual bosom of a community of people would join together to protect rather than destroy an innocent child. I grew up among a deeply spiritual people who chose to see me with their hearts instead of their eyes.

My mother, whose unanswered cries for help resulted in her alcoholism and the abuse of her children, also taught me to be in awe of knowledge and embrace learning with all of my heart. Even under these adverse conditions, my mother managed to give me that one gift I would never be able to measure: like the universe, the value of learning is infinite.

In light of the recent Los Angeles riots, there is an urgent necessity for people like myself who grew up in the ghetto to become a voice that speaks out to America to help this nation better understand the complex web of gripping problems that entrap most ghetto children.

I will take you on a journey into the ghetto where a brutal reality becomes a normal part of life in the minds and hearts of the children who are forced to experience it. In a soil rarely watered or touched by the warmth of the sun, these tiny wildflowers emerge through the cracks of a cement sidewalk. For a brief moment they blossom, unnoticed, everywhere you walk.

※ ※

Fifteen is a difficult age for anyone . . . a time when we not only want to belong, we *need* to belong. It is a stage in our lives when we are practicing how to become men and women. Our mentors are the adults that surround us. When those adults belong to a different culture and race than our own, the process of developing into a man or a woman takes a very interesting turn.

This is my story: a young White girl who was, by the age of fifteen, fully adopted into the Mexican culture. I had already spent nine years of my life almost completely isolated from my own race.

In elementary school, most of the children were Black; I became very comfortable with Black children. At Hollenbeck Junior High and Roosevelt High School, most of the children were Mexican. During roll call, the myriad of Spanish names became so familiar that the sound of my own last name began to sound unnatural.

Perhaps the monumental thing that kept drawing me closer to the Mexican culture was their warmth and love of children ... warmth that was so absent in my own home ... warmth for which my heart had been hunting since my father had abandoned me. I did not really understand all of this at the time. It was not a thought but a feeling that pulled me right into the bosom of the Mexican culture.

This is where my story really begins. A journey implies motion. If life is really a journey, then it is necessary for life to always remain in motion. So it was with my journey into the Mexican culture. Life does not stand still for anyone. I was destined to follow my journey to its conclusion.

* *

I sat on the back porch, gazing out at the cloudy sky. My mind was occupied with the thought of how to appear older. I wanted to get a job working in a Los Angeles theater selling popcorn, hot dogs and soda ... a *real* job, unlike baby-sitting. There was one obstacle: I needed to be sixteen to acquire a work permit.

Later that afternoon I boarded a bus for downtown Los Angeles. As I reached my destination, I stepped out of the bus and disappeared into the crowds of people. I eyed the ominous department store that stood before me and wondered if all the money I had saved from baby-sitting, securely tucked away inside my purse, could buy a single item in such a magnificent store.

I pulled open one of the heavy glass, main entrance doors and timidly stepped inside to an array of glass cases that seemed to be housing the world's supply of perfume and makeup.

Ever so carefully, I approached one of the counters. A young woman — impeccably dressed, freshly cut and styled hair, makeup perfectly applied — inquired what I would like to see. As I quickly eyed the rows and piles of small boxes and bottles that lined the glass shelves, I politely said, "I would like to look at a bottle of face makeup," desperately trying to sound as though all this came naturally to me.

The saleswoman pulled out a bottle and smeared a small dab of the beige hue across my wrist. Like an unexpected flash of lightning, that darker pigment against my pale white wrist triggered a secret desire, unbeknownst and unplanned. As the saleswoman began to reach for a lighter shade of makeup, I announced, "I'll take the shade you just showed me."

"That shade is far too dark for you, my dear."

It was as though someone else were moving my lips. "I have been very ill. That is why I look so pale. My natural complexion is much darker than this." The saleswoman looked very perplexed as she placed the darker shade of makeup in a bag and handed it to me.

Feelings flooded me all at once: I did not really feel White anymore; my Mexican and Black friends and their families accepted and emotionally embraced me; they stood by me when I needed them. What had White people ever done for me except make me feel sorry I was ever born?

My White grandfather and grandmother, as well as my own father, had completely abandoned me — just threw me away like a piece of trash. My White foster mother had brutally mistreated both me and my little brother. My Jewish mother, due to her own problems, was forced to reject and emotionally abandon me. All of the White adults with whom I had ever had a personal relationship had severed their affection from me in one way or another. Why should I want to be White?

I did not decide to emotionally abandon my own race without a reason; I had a long list of very sound reasons. The problem was that you can never be what you are not — to try is the greatest form of self-hatred. It is a one-way street to an emotional dead end. This is why minorities have fought so hard to maintain their cultures and identities.

It is not until we learn to respect and accept our own race, and therefore ourselves, that we can truly learn to respect and love others of another race. Self-hatred and lack of self-respect provide the foundation upon which racism is developed in people, and is perpetuated from one generation to another. Something inside dies when you feel the need to reject who you are in order to accept yourself. You lose something precious and the road back to recovery is a long and arduous one.

In order to truly understand my story and my feelings, we have to go back to a place and time when I had no knowledge of abandonment and betrayal . . . a time when I was free to feel like a child . . . a time when the ghetto was a million miles away . . .

PART I

Runaway Father:
Throwaway Children

1

Children Have No Voice

The scent of bananas still lingers in my memory. I sat on a tall stool with long, gangly legs dangling over the sides. My grandmother reached into her kitchen cabinet, pulled out a box wrapped in pink ribbons and bows, and whispered, "It's for you!"

Excitedly, I tore away the fancy wrappings to discover a pink-and-white checked gingham dress buried beneath piles of soft tissue. I held the dress in front of me and indicated to my grandmother that I would like to try it on. With a generous hug, my grandmother folded me in her arms and carried me off into her bedroom. She helped me remove the clothes I was wearing and slip into the dress she made especially for me.

As I peered into the mirror and admired my new dress, I suggested that we have our picture taken. My grandfather snapped the black-and-white photograph and wrote "4 YRS OLD" on the back. I still have it and cherish it to this day.

When I was four years old in 1957, we lived next door to my father's parents in a very nice one-story home with a spacious backyard. The backyard is far more clear in my memory than the

3

inside of the house. I spent many long hours playing among the fruit trees my grandfather had planted. They towered far above me — I pretended they were castles. I climbed the trees and envisioned myself to be a princess looking out across far-reaching, lush green meadows and pastures. In my mind I invented grazing white sheep and golden brown cows as the wind gently blew their tails back and forth.

When I was not playing in the backyard, I played with my dolls. There was a doll in my collection that I loved more than all the rest; my father gave it to me for my fourth birthday. The doll was dressed in a beautiful long, white satin gown and tiny white shoes adorned her feet; a veil of lace cascaded down her shoulders.

My father explained to me that this doll was different because she was a bride, and when little girls are very good they grow up to be beautiful brides someday. My eyes widened with wonder as the enchanting dream swirled through my mind. On a small shelf above my bed, I pushed my other dolls to both ends and my new bride doll occupied a special place of honor.

One morning my father brought home Easter baskets. I heard him scampering about the kitchen as I slowly tiptoed out of bed. I curiously peeked in past the doorway of the kitchen to find my father playfully hiding the baskets in various places. Pastel-tinted cellophane generously covered each basket where a soft, furry bunny surrounded by candies and small toys nestled inside.

My brother Mike and I were always put to bed following a round of horsy-back rides: we straddled my father's back while he circled around the room countless times on all fours. The best game of all was when I stood on top of a dresser and leaped into the air, as though I were Peter Pan, always landing in the waiting arms of my father.

You could often find me in the shelter of my father's lap, curled up closely to him, while the other children played nearby. However, my father's imperfections were often transparent to me when he exploded into anger at the slightest provocation.

I can still hear the biting words and see the piercing glances on one afternoon. He and his father were fighting about the fruit trees my grandfather planted in our backyard. My grandfather expressed his strongly held belief that all children should have trees in their backyard; I wholeheartedly agreed. My grandfather went on to inform my father that he paid a lot of money for those trees.

In response, my father complained that the fruit trees in our backyard attracted too many flies. Regarding the cost of the trees, my father shrugged his shoulders and defiantly announced his intention to give them away for *free*. My grandfather stormed out of our backyard, swearing under his breath.

The following day I forlornly watched two trucks take my "castles" away. All the wonderful moments I spent in those trees played over in my mind. As the trucks drove away, I noticed my grandmother walking towards our house. As she entered our backyard she greeted me with a warm smile and a hug. She walked over to my father and confronted him about the trees.

The fury in his eyes could only be matched by the rage that rang out in his voice. "Whose damn trees are they anyway, *mine or yours?*"

With those words, my grandmother was reduced to tears. She rushed out of our backyard as my father angrily glared at her. It was the first time I witnessed my father's wrath being played out towards his mother. It was a chilling experience to watch the people you love treat each other with so much animosity.

Many years later, I learned to understand the hostility that surrounded my father's family. My grandmother, a nursing student of German and Irish descent, lived in Panama when she was a very young woman. During the course of a romantic relationship with a man named Jack Brencheck, a child was conceived. Shortly afterwards my grandmother was abandoned and forced to bear this child alone.

The father later returned to claim rights to his son. His actions indicated a deep regret for what he did and sought forgiveness. Embittered, my grandmother vowed that he would never know or see his son. She blocked his every attempt and in the end her will prevailed.

When the child reached the age of two, my grandmother married a man named Malden Grange Bishop. He adopted and

raised the little boy as his own. At the insistence of my grandmother, the child was never told that Malden Grange Bishop was
not his natural father.

Malden Bishop was a technical writer who provided well for his
family. When his children wanted a car, he bought them one; when
they wanted a house, he gave them one. At eighteen the young
man joined the army. When he was required to show a birth
certificate, he was mistakenly issued the original instead of the
updated version. Completely unprepared for what he was about to
discover, he learned that the man he always believed to be his
natural father was, in fact, his *adopted* father.

The experience dramatically transformed him; he would never
again be the same person. When the dust finally settled, he was left
with an unopened door: he had to find his natural father.

Driven by a fierce determination, he discovered many things.
He found out for the first time that his natural father made many
attempts to see him when he was a child. He also learned that
those attempts were blocked and kept secret by his mother. He
hired a private detective and invested a great deal of time and
money to ascertain knowledge and the possible whereabouts of his
natural father. When he finally located him he discovered, much
to his despair, that his father was already in the grave. He collapsed
with overwhelming grief at the sight of his father's grave. Like a
man completely defeated, he cried out in agony for the father he
was never allowed to know.

From that point on, my grandparents recognized that he was a
deeply troubled person and felt heavily responsible for his personal problems. However, to their dismay, their past actions already
determined his fate and that of his unborn children.

He became a person who mindlessly produced children for
the sole purpose of acting out the tragedy that had once been his
childhood. He chose to victimize his own children in a far more
severe manner than his parents had victimized him. He achieved
this by marrying two unsuspecting women and placing them in the
same vulnerable position as his mother was before his birth. He
abandoned each woman during her weakest moment for the pur-

pose, it seemed, of inflicting the maximum amount of pain. One of those women was my mother.

My father was about nineteen when he married his first wife; they quickly had two children. Shortly after the birth of the second child, my father deserted them. My grandparents took care of his first wife and her two children until she remarried.

My father married my mother in his mid-twenties. On August 13, 1953 in Ogden, Utah, I was the first born of five children. I was named after my legal paternal grandfather's sister Kathleen and my mother's older sister Muriel, who died in a car accident before I was born.

My brother Michael Malden was born on August 18, 1954 in Culver City, California, and was named after our legal paternal grandfather Malden Grange Bishop. My sister Patricia was born on May 27, 1956 in San Francisco, California, and was named after our paternal grandmother. My sister Carrie Ann was born on May 29, 1957 in Lynwood, California, and was named after our aunt Ann, our father's only sister and sibling. Carrie was born during the time we lived next door to my grandparents.

I recall my aunt Ann hurrying over to see Carrie and cradling her tiny, squirming body. My aunt Ann had tried several times to bear children. Every pregnancy, even those where she reached five months, ended in a miscarriage. Her husband Bob could no longer stand to watch her agonize through one pregnancy after another and finally convinced her to adopt. Because Bob was Mexican, they decided to choose a child that was half Mexican and half Irish: an eighteen-month-old little girl named Delita.

One afternoon, as I was playing in my uncle Bob's kitchen with Delita, I heard my uncle Bob tell my dad (who was also called Bob) about an incident at work where someone made an unflattering remark about Mexicans. The experience had really shaken my uncle Bob.

Suddenly, my father sat further back in the tilted kitchen chair beneath him. He lifted the dark-colored bottle of beer in his hand and angrily announced, "Most people are full of shit. They don't know their ass from a hole in the ground. Why do you give a *damn* what these assholes think? I say to hell with them *all.* That's what you should do."

My uncle Bob's face conveyed a look of surprise at the deeply felt conviction in my father's voice. (Keep in mind that, in addition to being born in Panama, my father spent the first five years of his life being taught Spanish by his playmates. Like most people, my father developed strong emotional attachments to the people that surrounded his early childhood.) Judging from the look on my uncle Bob's face, he had never encountered a person like my father. I could see that my uncle Bob was deeply touched by my father's genuine feelings of affection for his people. However, that observation seemed to go right over my father's head; he was never aware of his emotional impact on other people.

My father was that unusual combination of strength and vulnerability that allows men to simultaneously command respect and exhibit affection. Unfortunately, he would allow his personal problems to rob him of a conscience. Like a fire that has the power to cook your food and warm your home — or burn your house down — my father would choose to use his natural gifts to destroy rather than enhance the lives of all those who loved him.

✳ ✳

When we returned home that evening from visiting my uncle Bob, my father unexpectedly announced that we were going to move to Denver, Colorado. My father held no discussion with my mother as she always passively submitted to my father's every whim. As a child, it was very clear to me who had the power in my family: my father was king and my mother was invisible.

A spacious veranda was attached to the old, two-story Victorian that was to become our new home in Denver. A short flight of stairs led up to the front door which was barely visible behind a metal-frame screened door. The front door faced a stairway that led up to a long hallway of bedrooms. Hidden underneath the stairway was a very tiny room in which all the children loved to play.

As you entered the front door to the right, a large living room opened up to a dining room. The kitchen was directly behind the dining room through a small doorway. Two large carpets covered the hardwood floors in the entrance way and the living room; the hardwood floor lay bare in the dining room. It was during this time that my mother conceived her fifth and last child due to be born in early October.

One bright, sunny morning I was playing in front of our house. I pulled out a stubble of chalk that I always carried around with me. As I drew the square boxes of my hopscotch and began to jump in them, I noticed a man on a ladder painting the house next door. I walked over to where he was working, introduced myself, and asked him if he would like to meet my mother.

He looked down at me with a broad smile. "Sure, I would like to meet your mother."

I raced over to my house and pulled my mother out by the hand onto our front porch. Her maternity smock hugged her large, round abdomen; her swollen ankles bulged over the sides of her widely spread feet, tightly stuffed into her flat-heeled shoes. I announced with unabashed pride, "This is my mother!" The man smiled warmly and my mother's face beamed with pride.

The following morning I woke up with the warm sun gently touching my face. Humming one of my favorite songs I bounced out of bed, slipped a bathrobe over my nightgown, and wiggled my feet into warm, furry slippers. I skipped along the hallway, carelessly running my hand along the wooden railing, when the sound of shattered glass broke my stride.

Cautiously, I ventured toward the downstairs kitchen and saw my father standing near the sink. His words pierced my ears as he roared at my mother, "I should never have married a damn *Jew!*" He further provoked my mother's anger as he flaunted his affair with another woman. I peered through the doorway as my mother stood at the other end of the kitchen, grasping a broken, jagged-edged bottle by the neck.

In a complete state of confusion and shock, I darted out in front of my mother. "Please don't hurt my daddy!" Instantly, my mother broke into tears and dropped the bottle into the kitchen sink. Its jagged edges were inches from my face.

I ran back upstairs to my room, my mind spinning out of control. I found comfort in the soft, familiar pillow that cushioned my head and rocked myself to sleep.

✳ ✳

The next morning, a heavy blanket of tension fell upon the living room as I watched my parents move about. Their expressionless faces, drained of all emotion, conveyed my greatest fear: losing one of my parents. An eerie feeling encroached upon my stomach when my father's eyes met mine and suddenly glanced away.

My eyes tenaciously followed his every move and facial expression as he dodged the horror in my face. Dread completely flooded me when my father approached the front door. I rushed towards him but he continued out of the door without stopping. I was stunned as I realized that I might never see him again and tightly clutched the screen door as though I could hold onto a tiny piece of the past.

There I stood, deeply desiring to pull open the door and race out after my daddy, pleading for his return. Paralyzed by the shock that my father could actually leave me, I was completely unable to move. All I could do was stand there as my whole life came to a screeching halt. As I helplessly watched my father step into his black Ford and start the engine, a deep sense of desperation engulfed me. His car faded into the distance; so did the world that had once belonged to my daddy and me.

That day at school, the minutes dragged on like hours as a dulling pain gnawed at me inside. All I desired was the sanctuary of my bedroom where my favorite and most cherished memories of my father still resided. The countless bedtime stories, fearless leaps through the air, and the horsy-back rides were vivid in my mind.

That afternoon, as I slowly lagged behind the other children on my way home from school, the roaring blast of an ambulance siren raced down our street. I looked on in horror as I realized that it was stopping in front of *my house*. As I ran towards it, I saw my mother being carried out on a stretcher. Her body was tightly bound with straps as she wept hysterically. Two men carried her to the ambulance and placed her inside.

As the ambulance began to drive away, I instinctively chased it until my legs grew so numb I could no longer feel them beneath me. My stride was suddenly broken by a sharp pain swelling up in my chest. Tears poured down my face and soaked my blouse collar as I hopelessly watched the ambulance turn and disappear from sight. A chilling dread choked me inside. I suddenly realized that I had lost both of my parents in one single day. As I headed back in the direction of my house, disparaging thoughts were quickly forming in my mind: *Where would we go? Who was going to take care of us?*

Completely oblivious to the situation, my two little sisters were rolling canned food across the hardwood floors as I entered the house. My little brother quietly sat slouched on the sofa with a deep sense of sorrow outlined on his tear-stained face. Each minute ticked louder than the one that preceded it as we waited for whatever was to be our fate. I felt as though the earth had suffered a giant earthquake and all that had been our lives was swallowed up in it. Like the scattered ruins left remnant following such an earthquake, fleeting memories were all that would remain.

✳ ✳

A loud knock at the front door summoned us into an unknown future and a complex set of circumstances that would drastically and forever change our lives. When I opened the door, two ladies from the Social Services Department rushed inside and hurriedly collected a few of our belongings. I dashed upstairs and pulled my bride doll down from her shelf — the comforting reminder and beacon of hope that my father might someday return.

All of us were taken to a large building that housed many small offices. We were placed in one of the offices and instructed to wait. A woman returned and casually announced that we would have to be separated; we instantly became a united front. Protectively, I pulled all of my siblings behind me and pleaded for a change in their decision. I painfully learned that we had *no voice* in the matter and no such change would be forthcoming.

Deep down in my soul I silently screamed, "How could they *do* this to us? We just lost both of our parents *in one single day*! How could anyone be so inhuman as to rip us away from each other on that very same day?"

However, without a second thought, that is exactly what they did. Devoid of any compassion or emotion, they simply shipped us off like cardboard boxes being sent to unknown destinations. My little brother and I were sent to one foster home and my two little sisters to another.

2

Behind Closed Doors

My brother Mike and I walked along a sidewalk where a row of well-kept homes were nestled behind neatly manicured green lawns. With my little brother tightly clutching my hand, we cautiously ventured closer to the front door of our new foster home; two social workers followed closely behind.

A middle-aged Caucasian woman greeted us and cheerfully invited us into her home. She kindly offered my brother and me cookies and milk in the kitchen. She returned to the living room where the two social workers were seated. Upon finalizing the papers necessary to receive payment for our care, she escorted the two social workers to the front door.

As soon as the social workers disappeared, our foster mother stormed into the kitchen. She angrily ordered us to wash dishes and sternly warned that if one speck of food remained on those dishes, we would be punished. As I studied her facial expression through the corner of my eye, I knew my brother and I were in trouble.

I tried to wash both of our dishes but our foster mother insisted that he do his own. His eyes looked up at me, silently begging for help. The nervous rattling of the dish he held in his hand made his shivering fear transparent. It slipped and loudly banged against the bottom of the empty kitchen sink.

Instantly, our foster mother stormed into the kitchen carrying a black rod in her hand. She struck my little brother repeatedly, covering his back and legs with large, red welts until he lay frantically sobbing on the kitchen floor.

Shortly after our foster mother's departure from the kitchen, I nervously peered through the door to make sure she was gone. I pulled my brother's swollen body into the tiny bedroom that had been designated for our use. That night my little brother crawled out of his bed and into mine. In the darkness, he curled up next to me and his body folded into a small, tight ball.

The following morning our foster mother appeared at the entrance of our bedroom and ordered us to get dressed. Panic-stricken, we frantically pulled and tugged at our clothes as we attempted to put them on at lightning speed. Following our tremendous effort to fulfill her wishes, our foster mother announced that we had failed and would have to incur a punishment. My brother, still aching from his beating on the previous day, huddled behind me in complete terror.

When we arrived home from school that afternoon we were immediately placed into a small, dark coat closet. As we began to sit down on the floor, our foster mother made it a stipulation that we stand and remain completely silent.

During our repeated stays in the pitch-black darkness of the tiny closet, I learned to occupy my mind by studying the texture of the walls with my fingers. I practiced calculating the tone and distance of the voices outside the closet. I groped for the thin slice of sunlight edging its way into the closet from beneath the door. It always felt as though a lifetime had slipped by before the door was again opened and we were released from our cramped prison.

One afternoon, our foster mother flew into a rage when she opened the closet door to discover my little brother, too tired to remain standing, sitting on the floor. She ran into the kitchen and returned with a heavy rope. She tautly wound the rope around my brother's knees, squeezing the reddened skin peeking out of the rope. She gripped the rope into a tight knot that rendered him unable to bend his knees to sit down.

* *

Kitchen and bathroom privileges had to be earned. If we made one sound in the closet, we lost dinner or one of our three daily trips to the bathroom. Mike found it much more difficult to be in the closet than I did because he was not old enough to figure out ways to occupy his mind.

On one warm afternoon he became fidgety and restlessly tossed his arms about, creating a slight noise. Instantly the door swung open. There stood our foster mother sternly assigning Mike his punishment: he would not be permitted his afternoon bathroom privilege. A short time later, the sweltering closet began to reek with the smell of urine. Again the closet door flung wide open as the bright afternoon sunlight painfully banged against our eyes.

Our foster mother roared, "You little piece of *filth!*" Immediately she yanked Mike from the closet and slammed the door with me still inside. The horrible stench cooking in the heat of the closet made me nauseous; I fought hard to prevent myself from vomiting for fear of being punished.

When my little brother returned to the closet, he was dressed in only a cloth diaper supported by two, large safety pins. A silhouette — his head hung down in shame and his shoulders hunched over in defeat — emerged in the darkness . . . like a drawing that silently speaks of a child's pain.

When we lost kitchen privileges, I often snuck into the kitchen very late at night and quietly stole food. I removed slices of bread from the center of each loaf and carefully repackaged the bread to its exact original appearance. From a block of tightly packed cheese, I peeled away a slice or two and repacked it to appear precisely as it was before. I became so adept that I stole complete meals without detection.

In spite of the fact that I knew the Social Services Department paid for the food I stole, I never felt good about stealing because my mother had taught me it was wrong to steal. I really had to grapple with those feelings in order to do what was necessary for the survival of my little brother and me.

One afternoon the closet door unexpectedly opened and our foster mother's daughter, who was much older than I, ordered me to step out. I hesitated to leave my little brother alone in the darkness but I had no choice. She handed me a book far beyond my ability to read and ordered me to read it. Slowly I opened the book and stumbled over the first word. Instantly, she grabbed a small handful of my long hair and ripped it from my scalp. I felt the warm blood slowly trickle down the back of my scalp and silently screamed out in agony. My tears were buried behind a blank face.

On another occasion, this same daughter removed the bride doll from my bedroom. She chastised me for my obvious attachment to the doll as she immersed her beautiful, white gown into the rotting garbage at the bottom of a large pail. My entire body shook with a frenzied rage and a deep, profound hatred formed in my heart.

That night, under a blanket of darkness, I found no sleep. The dark had become my light; I played with the animal shadows I created with my fingers on the bedroom wall. I made the darkness my friend and the light my enemy.

**

An unexpected phone call from my mother came one afternoon. Our foster mother warned that she would be listening in on the extension. Her voice, still weak from a stress-induced delivery and complete nervous breakdown, faintly announced that I had a new baby brother named William Clayton, named after my legal paternal grandfather's father, William Clayton Bishop. When my mother added that he would be coming to our foster home to stay with us, I gasped in horror at the thought. The mouthpiece of the phone almost slipped from my hand.

Two social workers delivered my baby brother to our foster home. I am happy to report that no harm came to him during his stay there.

On the morning my mother arrived to pick us up, we rushed out the front door without saying a word. My mother prompted me to thank our foster mother for the care she had provided; my face could only register a blank stare. There was not a soul on this earth that could have made me thank that woman for the wrath Mike and I were forced to incur under her care. For the first time in my six years of life, I learned to hate another human being.

3

Aliso Village

Two social workers drove us to a train station where we were reunited with my little sisters. Pat came rushing up to my mother; Carrie lagged far behind her. As my mother reached to embrace both of them, Carrie quickly retreated back to her foster mother . . . she had forgotten who her real mother was.

Pat stepped right in to set the record straight. They had always been like twins, being only a year and two days apart; wherever Pat went, Carrie went. So, as we boarded the train, Carrie reluctantly followed Pat to her seat. Chugging along slowly at first, the train rapidly picked up speed.

We were destined for Los Angeles, California and arrived on a chilly morning. When we disembarked, the Welfare Department failed to meet us. With four small children trailing behind and a six-week-old infant bundled in her arms, my mother was forced to knock on doors asking someone to help us. An Oriental woman took us in, gave us shelter for a few nights, and referred us to a nearby mission where we stayed a few more nights. The mission provided us with a large, clean room and a double-sized bed. No heating, blankets or sheets were available. It was November 1959.

Heavily bundled in several baby blankets, my mother placed Billy into a cardboard box and positioned him high on a closet shelf to avoid any cold draft that might touch him during the night. Nestled beneath my mother's big, warm winter coat, my two little sisters, my little brother and I fell asleep.

In the dining room the following morning, a clear broth soup sparsely ladened with noodles was served. My mother explained that we should be appreciative for the food and shelter that were provided, and that these things were given for free by people who really cared about children.

The following day we visited the Welfare Department. Their explanation for failing to show up was that we simply did not qualify for welfare. My legal paternal grandfather had been con- tacted and had agreed to support us with one stipulation: my mother would be required to relinquish legal custody of all five of her children to my grandfather. She vehemently refused.

The Welfare Department was completely unsympathetic to my mother's predicament and strongly advised her to relinquish all legal custody if she could not afford to support us. In desperation, my mother loudly threatened to go down to the *Los Angeles Times* and give them this story: "The Welfare Department of Los Angeles put a woman and her five children, including an infant, out on the street."

I remember people suddenly jumping out of their chairs to sign up my mother for welfare. A young Black man and woman then escorted us to a housing project called Aliso Village.

* *

The first day I entered Aliso Village I could feel the bleakness of the drab, pale green, three-story brick buildings that towered far above me. As I approached what would become my home for over a decade, an invisible iron gate seemed to close behind me, shut- ting me away from the rest of the world I had once known. The numbers "889" and the letter "D" marked the metal front door of our apartment; our street address was 137 Via Nicola.

The young Black woman from the Social Services Department took a special interest in me. I had never seen Black people before my arrival to Los Angeles. Even though her skin color appeared strange, her gentle eyes and warm voice beckoned my trust.

I was startled when she affectionately inquired what I wanted for Christmas. For the first time in my life, I had forgotten all about Christmas. My recently acquired experiences had erased that feeling of excitement and awe that inspired the spirit of Christmas in most children. I could only feel the cold stillness of a grave in my heart where my old life was freshly buried. A dull, sickening feeling haunted me; faded images of the past wandered far from my reach in the deep recesses of my mind.

✷ ✷

The following morning, I reluctantly ventured outside and pulled a stubble of chalk from my pocket. Slowly I drew one box at a time on the cement sidewalk that bordered our front lawn until all the squares of my hopscotch were completed. For a brief moment, as I jumped into the familiar squares, I felt as though I were back home in front of our house in Denver . . . I could hear my father calling my name.

My daydream was suddenly interrupted when a small group of Black girls approached me. One of them stroked my reddish-blonde hair and commented, "Girl, you sure got *good hair!*" Her choice of words sounded strange as all of them came rushing at me, stroking and touching my hair. (My mother always taught me to keep my hands to myself because it was impolite to touch people you did not know.) I turned around and walked away from these girls thinking they were being rude. However, that was not how *they* perceived it.

The following morning was my first day of school. My mother taught me how to cross the street using the underground tunnel on First Street. As I slowly approached it, the group of Black girls that had stroked my hair the previous day followed me underneath the dark tunnel. When I was about halfway through, they ran towards me and kicked and punched me several times.

I screamed hysterically as they quickly fled through the other end of the tunnel, abandoning me in the darkness. I raced home and rushed through the front door. Talking through my tears, I was able to identify one of the girls who lived upstairs on the opposite side of us.

My mother went to discuss the incident with her mother. When my mother returned, she informed me that the daughter I had identified had been there with her mother. She said the little girl denied ever hitting me that morning.

My mother proceeded to pull out an army belt that once belonged to my father. She struck me with it as she yelled, "Negroes have it so hard in this world and no one understands that better than me, because I am a Jew. I will not have any of my children falsely accusing Negroes of crimes they did not commit!" I felt my anger swell as my mother repeatedly struck me for telling the truth. I quickly grew numb and images of my foster mother beating Mike took form in my mind.

As my anger began boiling over into rage, there was a knock at the door. My mother opened the door and there stood the little girl from upstairs. Her mother was standing behind, hitting her with an extension cord. "You tell Mrs. Bishop the truth right now, girl, 'fore I whoop your behind some *more!*" The mother stood there with angry eyes, glaring at her daughter Sandra.

Through her sobs, the little girl confessed to beating me up with her friends and apologized to my mother and me. When my mother asked her why she and her friends beat me up, she simply said, "We thought she didn't like us!" Sandra and I would later become close friends.

4

Survival of the Fittest

Desperation echoed from my mother's voice as she spoke to someone at County Hospital for the fourth time that evening. "Something is wrong with my baby!"

I looked into the bassinet to see my baby brother Billy gasping for air as rattling noises erupted from his small chest. A tinge of blue was beginning to form on his pale, white skin; his arms and legs lay unnaturally still.

My mother hung up the phone and dialed another number. Tears ran down her face as panic rang out in her voice. "Please drive me to County Hospital! They will not send an ambulance. Please come or *my baby will die!*"

I hurriedly put on my coat, determined to accompany my mother and baby brother to the hospital. In less than ten minutes, there was a knock on the front door and three Black women rushed into our apartment. Two of them stayed with my siblings and one of them drove my mother, my little brother and me to the hospital.

The woman driving the car kept turning to examine the rapidly deteriorating condition of my baby brother, now making muffled sounds through his labored breathing. She sped through red lights and stop signs, loudly honking her car horn and hoping the other drivers would realize that this was an emergency.

Suddenly we were at County Hospital. My mother ran from the car with my baby brother in her arms; the woman and I ran behind her. Upon entering the emergency entrance, my baby brother stopped breathing. My mother screamed out in terror as a nurse rushed over and ripped my brother from my mother's arms. The nurse frantically began tearing off his clothes and ran down the corridor to place him in an oxygen tent. The Black woman who drove us to the hospital left.

My mother and I were asked to go to a waiting room. A short time later, the nurse returned and announced to my mother that my little brother had acute pneumonia; however, he was able to breathe again with the assistance of the oxygen tent. The deep sigh of relief that appeared on my mother's haggard face swiftly disappeared when the nurse added, "Mrs. Bishop, your son has only a fifty-fifty chance of surviving through the night." My mother instantly sank into a deep state of shock; her eyes became empty sockets drained of all emotion.

For a brief moment, images of my mother's gentle hands, patiently guiding me through the first needle I had ever threaded, softly lingered in my mind. It was a small but precious memory, now woven into a faded past I could no longer touch, smell or feel. My little brother survived that night but something inside of my mother did not.

5

The Black Box

The wide open window in my first grade classroom yielded a refuge. White puffs of cotton floated along an endless blue sea as I gazed out at the sky. I yearned to float freely like those clouds or be endless like that sky.

Even though my mother and my first grade teacher were standing only a few feet away from me, their voices faded in and out. The only part that I clearly heard was when my teacher warned my mother that I was in danger of failing the first grade.

My first grade teacher was a Black woman named Mrs. Gaylord. She was warm and nurturing but I was too afraid to respond to her on a daily basis. On many occasions she would attempt to converse with me. I found it extremely difficult to trust anyone with the one precious thing I had managed to salvage — my feelings.

Mrs. Gaylord slowly began to recognize that something was wrong with me and recommended psychological testing. The following week I was led out of my classroom by two adults I had never seen before. (I believe they were child psychologists.) I was escorted into a tiny, windowless room where I sat at a table pushed against a wall. When the lights went off, I imagined the tiny room to be the foster home closet.

A projector came on and I briefly allowed myself to be fascinated by the black silhouettes of cartoon characters that danced and skipped across the wall. Like a fetus rolled up into a tight ball and safely packed inside its mother's womb, I suddenly withdrew into myself. No one was going to push me out into this brutal world ever again! I refused to respond to the two adults in the room. Silence was the only protection I knew; I had learned to use it well.

When the lights came back on, a sense of panic overwhelmed me as I fought hard to hide the myriad of feelings all tangled up inside. The world now appeared a deadly place where people measured your vulnerability and exploited you accordingly.

One of the psychologists suggested that I draw some pictures. A pile of blank, white paper and a box of crayons were placed in front of me. (There would be several meetings before I finally complied with their request to draw.) A deep feeling of relief rushed through me as the two psychologists left me alone.

I picked up the box of crayons and opened the top to examine the colors. I first selected the warm, yellow crayon and drew a giant, glowing ball of light on the upper right-hand corner of the paper. Next, I pulled a black crayon from the carton without thought or examination. As I began drawing, images of my little brother emerged in my mind.

I could see the tight rope squeezing his bare flesh and his eyes wincing with pain. The faint splinters of sunlight sharply contrasting the tiny, dark space within the closet prompted me to draw a black box where two small children were trapped. In the cramped corner of that tiny prison, I learned to extinguish my feelings in order to protect my mind from the flood of pain that constantly threatened to destroy it.

I put the crayon down as one of the psychologists suddenly returned and sat down next to me. I felt as though I had awoken from a nightmare that left me very badly shaken. The psychologist sat closer which only enhanced my feelings of uneasiness.

He pulled the drawing closer to me and pointed to the bright yellow circle in the upper right-hand corner. I was asked to explain what it was . . . that was simple. Next, the psychologist examined the black box for a brief moment before he spoke. When he asked me what it was, I reluctantly revealed that it was a closet. His uneasy glance conveyed that I gave him the wrong answer to a commonly posed question. With piqued interest, the psychologist inquired why there were two people in the closet.

I whispered, "They are being punished."

The psychologist suddenly moved closer to me. "Why are you whispering?"

I responded in a faint voice, "She might hear me."

"*Who* might hear you?" The words felt trapped behind my lips as I struggled to say them. (I was absolutely certain that my foster mother would reappear at any moment to punish me.) "Who are you afraid of?"

In a barely audible, hushed voice, I finally responded, "My foster mother."

The psychologist's body stiffened in his chair as he continued to jot down notes on his clipboard. His eyes narrowed. "Who is the other person in the closet with you?"

"My little brother." When asked about the lines drawn across my little brother's legs, dread filled the psychologist's eyes as I explained that they were ropes used to prevent him from sitting down.

With grave concern, the psychologist asked about the small, white triangle drawn on my brother. I explained that it was the diaper used to punish him for having an accident in the closet because he was denied bathroom privileges. The psychologist's eyes held a look of bewilderment as he continued to record my story on his clipboard. That was the end of our sessions.

I barely functioned academically to pass the first grade. In my teens, my mother told me that she had been informed by Utah Elementary School that I was diagnosed, as a result of my meetings with the psychologists, as suffering from a nervous breakdown.

Part II

Shattered Innocence:
The Crime That Is
Never Brought To Justice

6

A Young Girl's Honor

I was so excited about spending the night at my friend Diane's house. It seemed a bit odd to me that she was being raised by her father rather than her mother. However, two much older sisters in their twenties also resided with them.

That night we popped popcorn, hit each other with pillows, and rolled all over the bed in laughter. It was midnight before we finally became sleepy. All the salt on the popcorn prompted our thirst; we silently tiptoed into the darkness from the bedroom to the kitchen.

Diane was standing directly in front of me, holding her glass beneath the running faucet. A hand from behind slipped into my pajama bottoms and touched my bottom. Terror-stricken, I turned to see her father's face outlined in the darkness.

I yanked his hand from my pajama bottoms and darted for the front door. Frantically, I unlocked it and burst out into the pitch-black night, sobbing hysterically. My bare feet pounded on the freezing cement as I dashed past Utah Elementary School towards

First Street. My heart was loudly banging in my chest and a stony chill struck my face.

I sprang into the large main street without regard for the light because the terror that engulfed me would not allow me to slow down. A car suddenly jolted to a stop — missing me by inches — and I came crashing down to the ground. Frozen with fear, I kept trying to reach for the curb and pull myself up without success.

A woman stepped out of the car that almost hit me. She pulled me up and asked if I was all right. (She could see that I was distraught and still sobbing.) She walked me to where I lived and waited for me to climb the stairs to my apartment.

I ran and pounded on the front door. "Mama! Mama! Mama! Mama!" When my mother finally answered the door, still groggy and half asleep, the woman that had walked me home was gone. I jumped into my mother's arms, still sobbing hysterically.

A mountain of confusion overwhelmed me as I stumbled over my words. An ocean of despair kept drowning me out every time I attempted to speak. After several hours I was able to relay to my mother bits and pieces of what had happened. I recall only being able to describe my experience as though it had happened to another little girl. I gave my mother a description of what the man did to the little girl and how the little girl ran away from the bad man.

My mother picked up the phone and called the Hollenbeck Police Department. The anger in her voice touched every part of the room as she relayed my story to the police. She insisted on filing criminal charges against this man. She stormed down to the police station the following day and did exactly that.

The Hollenbeck Police Department treated my mother and the incident as though it were a joke. They took my mother's report and just filed it away. Slowly, my mother's anger began to develop into a deep and lingering frustration — heavily contributing to her eventually becoming an alcoholic.

For years following that incident, I had a recurring dream: I was lying on a street, reaching for the curb. I had an intense desire to pull myself up but was completely unable to move. Cars and people would race right past, unable to hear or see me.

✳✳

As the terror of the night became more distant with time, I turned twelve. I was so proud to finally be a junior high school student. At the beginning of the year, I contracted laryngitis and temporarily lost my voice, keeping me home from school.

During that period, my mother spent time with the only man she ever dated while we lived in Aliso. He came over one morning when I was home and casually smiled at me as he walked through the door. My mother asked him if he would stay with me while she ran out to buy my medication. He agreed without hesitation and my mother left.

I was sitting on the couch watching television with my robe over my pajamas. The man quietly sat down on the couch next to me. When he began to move closer, I became very uncomfortable but said nothing out of politeness. I thought maybe he just wanted me to think of him as a father; maybe he just wanted to sit closer to me so we could watch television together like a family.

All of a sudden, one of his hands was on my thigh and he pushed his other hand under my nightgown, all the way up my legs. Panic-stricken, I leaped up from the couch, raced over to the bathroom and immediately locked the door. (It was the only room in our apartment with a lock.)

The bathroom door began to sound like thunder as the man vigorously pounded on it. I was petrified that the only thing standing between me and my fate may come crashing down at any moment.

His screaming words grew louder and louder inside my mind: "Open this door, you little *tramp!*" My eyes raced around the room, frantically searching for an escape and fighting hard not to let my terror overwhelm my ability to think. I pulled off the screens from the tiny window in the upper left-hand corner of the room and opened both windows as far as they would go. Uncertain that I would be able to push through such a tiny window, I wedged into the opening and positioned myself to jump the very moment the door swung open. (My mother once explained that there was a way to jump without breaking your legs. I fought hard to remember

what she said but my mind was succumbing to the terror screaming inside of me.)

I felt the warm tears pouring down my face when I heard my
mother enter the apartment. Like a soft, heavy blanket on a cold
winter's night, relief suddenly wrapped itself around me and began to smother the flames of panic that burned inside. My mother
ran into the bathroom as the man ran out the front door; she then
put me to bed.

A young girl's honor is fragile like a delicate piece of glass:
once shattered into tiny pieces, it can never be fully restored. A
deep sense of betrayal and disbelief at what my mother had just
witnessed prompted her to file with the Hollenbeck Police Department a report against this man. For a second time, nothing was
done!

Two men had violated and attacked my honor before I was
thirteen years of age. When reported to the police, neither was
required to pay a price for his actions nor have his crime brought
to justice.

There is a joke in the ghetto about the word "justice." It means
"just us" — meaning there is only justice for those outside the
ghetto. Children learn what they live. When they learn that it is a
joke when others violate them, they logically conclude that their
violation of others is equally a joke.

7

The Discovery of Love

In 1963 my grandfather, Malden Grange Bishop, wrote *The Discovery of Love* *, a book about his experiences as a volunteer used for a medical study on the effects of LSD.

One of my sisters found this book in a college library. When I read it, I discovered for the first time that my father had been previously married, fathered two children and had abandoned that family just as he did ours. I was hurt more than I was shocked; it was such a painful reminder of how disturbed my father really was.

My grandfather spent nine hours in a room experiencing LSD while music was played. All the patients were asked to bring pictures of family members and anything else that held meaning for them.

When my father's picture was held up, my grandfather described my father in these words: "Real good-looking guy. Happy-

---

* Bishop, Malden Grange. *The Discovery of Love*. P. 23, 136-138, New York: Dodd, Mead & Company, 1963.

go-lucky smile. Seems to be saying, Okay Pop let's go. I wonder if he understood that I loved him. I think he did. That's what he's saying now. Yeah. That something we have is still there. We have a feeling. I don't care what he's done or is, that's my boy!"

This is my grandfather's interpretation of my father following his experience with LSD: "When Bobby deserted his first wife and two children I was deeply disappointed. When I learned that he owed a mountain of debts, which he would never pay, I was sometimes angry, and sometimes ashamed. My pride was crushed that he had walked out on his responsibilities as a husband, a father, and a citizen. And when he repeated the pattern with the second wife and children I was again deeply hurt. Still I never stopped loving him.

"Gradually, as my anger cooled, as I forgot my pride, I came to understand that Bobby had a freedom which I did not have. He was able to stand above and beyond, rightfully or wrongfully, morals, conventions, and laws. I have often wanted that same sort of freedom. I do not want to violate moral codes, social conventions, or legal regulations just to be violating them. I am in favor of these as long as they serve a good purpose. But it is common sense that when our codes, conventions, and laws become our masters they are no good. They must help us toward God, not restrict us. They must help us to grow, to mature, not stifle and deaden us. Love can only survive in freedom.

"Whether Bobby was casting off the right laws, customs and morals I do not know. I do know that he had the courage to free himself of whatever seemed to restrict him in his inner self. He did it without regard to, or maybe in spite of, any condemnation which came from society, from friends, from loved ones. Bobby claimed for himself, and took, the same kind of freedom an artist claims to express himself with nude paintings, four-letter words in a book, strange melodies in a piece of music, strange forms in sculpture.

"Bobby claimed for himself the same freedom of choice which Martin Luther claimed when he rebelled against the established church and touched off the Protestant Movement; that Henry Miller took when he wrote his *Tropic of Cancer* and *Tropic of Capricorn*; that our forefathers took when they established a new nation dedicated to the proposition that 'all men are created equal'; that the rebels of all times have taken to mark something wrong in the present, and to point to something more right in the future.

"What Bobby was saying to me in, 'Come on, Pop, let's go,' was an invitation to come and join him in letting go of all the old and unnatural morals, conventions, and laws to which I have so long submitted myself. To come on and 'let's go' into a future free of these fetters, chains, and irons. This is exactly what I have wanted to do but have never had the full courage to do. I have wanted to be liberated, I wanted a freedom, and Bobby was telling me to take it.

"Instead of being the happy-go-lucky boy I thought, instead of being the irresponsible, carefree, immoral, unconventional, lawless one, Bobby was the most serious person I have ever known. A man must be deeply serious to have the courage to stand against the awesome power of organized society. Bobby cared a lot. He was being responsible to basic and natural laws far more important than any enacted by man. Morals and conventions change from day to day. Legal rules are repealed and new ones made each day. All these things are temporary. But the morals, the conventions, the laws to which Bobby was responding are eternal. I am very glad that Bobby is my boy."

* *

During 1963, when my grandfather wrote this noble description of my father, I — Bobby's own daughter and Malden Grange Bishop's granddaughter — was sexually assaulted. Where was my father who should have been there to protect my honor? My grandfather mentions in his book that my father was being responsible to basic and natural laws far more important than any enacted by man. I ask you: what is more basic and natural to a man than his desire to protect the honor *of his own daughter*? My father did not even possess that basic and natural instinct common to most men.

In his book, my grandfather boasts of his financial worth. "Economically I had prospered fairly well. I lived in a $50,000 house, which had no mortgage on it. Without the aid of a college degree, important relatives, or influential friends, I had bank and savings accounts amounting to five figures, and my Dunn and Bradstreet balance sheet showed a net worth of more than $100,000.00." (Keep in mind that this was 1963 when the price of an average home was only about $20,000.)

In the midst of all this prosperity, he allowed his own grandchildren to grow up condemned to suffer the humiliation and stigma of welfare. My grandfather had to have full, legal custody of all five of us or have nothing to do with any of us. This is a man who claims to love humanity, yet he could not find enough compassion in his own heart to rescue his grandchildren from the hideous circumstances that surround the lives of all ghetto children.

My grandfather says that my father had the courage to stand against the awesome power of society. What kind of courage does it take for a man to abandon four small children and a woman who is eight months' pregnant?

It is ironic that the courage on which my grandfather placed such a high value did not belong to him or his son. It belonged instead to the five small children who were abandoned and forced to develop, like all ghetto children, *real* courage in order to survive.

8

A Crime Committed Against a Child

There was a record shop inside an old, rust-colored brick building located on Boyle Heights. A paint-blistered doorway led into the shop. My friends and I brushed our way past the teenagers that were always crowded in and around the entrance. Gum loudly popped and smacked to the beat of the tune being played. Records hanging from rusty nails lined the walls, safely secured behind the counter.

One of my friends asked if a copy of "I'm Your Puppet" was available. Her eyes twinkled as the salesgirl nodded and slipped the last copy into a small, thin bag. As the salesgirl wrote out a receipt, I recognized a girl standing in the far left corner of the record shop. She was the one that always ran around Aliso on the cold, winter pavement — barefoot and without a jacket. (Children in Aliso did not have much, but most did have a pair of shoes and a winter jacket.)

Huddled in the corner of the record shop with her arms tightly folded across her chest, I noticed a faint trickle of tears meandering down her cheeks. I was thirteen and she was fifteen; I felt inadequate to offer my support or friendship.

About four months later, I saw her walking through Aliso with the very round abdomen of an expectant mother. I understood then the tears and pain I saw in her eyes that day in the record shop. Several times during her pregnancy, she passed near my apartment. I took the opportunity one day to speak to her and we began having brief conversations.

During the course of her pregnancy, I learned that the father of her baby was the same man that lived upstairs from me, next door to Sandra. (He was also the one that conducted prostitution parties in his apartment.) I also sadly learned that he had offered her $5 to have sex with him. In light of her extreme childhood depravation, which had badly damaged her self-perception, this beautiful young girl accepted his absurd offer.

When her little girl was born I came to visit, eager to hold the tiny infant in my arms. Her nose and mouth were perfectly formed and beautifully framed by a head full of soft curls. I asked if I could take her home for a short while to show her off to my mother.

A deep sense of sadness overwhelmed me when this young mother looked up and bitterly remarked, "You can *keep* her if you want to." I quietly wrapped the baby in a warm blanket and said I would be back in a few hours.

∗ ∗

In the eyes of the law, this situation would have been defined as statutory rape had it taken place outside the ghetto — clearly not the act of two consenting adults. Rather, it was the act of an adult detestably exploiting the tragic dilemma of a young girl's life. It was a brutal act of violence perpetrated against a child because she lacked the emotional development to defend herself and the societal support to protect her against this hideous crime.

The essence of this story goes even deeper than the crime. What happens to the innocent child that was born out of this tragedy? What kind of force does it take to shape a young girl's mind into believing that her precious body should be handed over to a drunken pimp for $5? What kind of power does it take to destroy the natural instinct of a mother to want to keep her newborn infant?

Part III

Special Friendships: Crossing Over The Line That Divides Races

9

Blood Sisters

I can still feel the sun as it bathed my seven-year-old face in its warmth that afternoon. The sweet scent of the tiny, red berries planted outside my school yard followed me. As I drew closer to home, I noticed a little girl I had not seen before.

The girl looked up to the second floor as her mother conversed in Spanish. She wore a Catholic school uniform with a crisp, white cotton blouse neatly tucked into a dark plaid skirt. The skirt was gathered at the waist and came down to her knees. Her dark, brown hair was combed into two perfectly symmetrical braids that gracefully cascaded down her shoulders. Her eyes were like two, brand new copper pennies shining in the sunlight. Our eyes met for the first time and a friendship was born. Angela was eight years old.

The depth of our friendship was slow to develop because of my mother. It was not anything my mother said; it was how she made me feel. I was learning what goes deeper than words: I should feel afraid of people who belong to a different race; not that they were inferior or superior, just different — compatible only as acquaintances.

In all fairness to my mother, I think she was only teaching me, on an emotional level, what she was taught as a child. I attempted to understand my mother's feelings; perhaps being a child did not allow me to see or understand the difference that was *supposed* to exist between Angela and me. I crossed over the line that held my mother back, and was rewarded with a friendship that would last throughout my childhood. The most descriptive way to describe Angela would be "full of adventure and fun."

∗ ∗

Our first skating adventure was to tease the old man who sat outside the Chinese theater on First Street. I was unsure about this escapade because of my lack of experience on skates, but Angela changed all that. Angela invited two other girls to join us.

We arrived at the theater and the playful teasing began. The little old man arose from his chair, shouted in Chinese and waved his cane. As we took flight on the steel wheels beneath our feet, the ground seemed to suddenly open up and I came crashing down on the cement.

Dumbfounded, I looked up in terror as the old man approached me. Perplexed by the hand he extended to help pull me up, I slowly and awkwardly skated away. Angela came racing towards me, like a protective older sister, to rescue me from my fate. I learned very quickly that I had to be fast on my skates to hang around with Angela and survive.

One of our next adventurous episodes was the pickle factory. Oh, the glee in Angela's eyes when she devised the elaborate plan for removing those juicy pickles from their barrels! She fashioned a hanger into a hook and attached it to a long broom handle. I stood on her shoulders as she balanced my body against the fence. Tenaciously, I gripped the broom handle attached to the hook, reached over to the top of the nearest pickle barrel, and tore it open. Instantly, the air was filled with the sour but delightful aroma of pickles. I gingerly guided the broom handle so that the hook on the end would sink deep down inside the tear and penetrate the flesh of the crisp pickle bathing in vinegar. Angela taught me how to feel, by the amount of resistance, when I should gently pull the broom handle. The pickles were so numerous in one barrel that the neighborhood kids stood in line as we distributed them.

Our next adventure was rock collecting. Angela and I loved to look for unusual rocks. The wide variety of shapes, colors and sizes fascinated us. We chose some small hills located behind the old Aliso housing projects, across the street from Utah Elementary School, and collected the most interesting rocks you have ever seen.

We took them to Angela's house and sorted them into groups according to shape, size, color and texture. Some were very smooth, oval and black with an almost mirror-like quality; others were milky and almost translucent, rough and magnificently speckled with bits of a golden hue. Angela and I cherished them as our treasures. We were always looking forward to our next exploration for new and different rocks so we could add them to our growing collection.

One afternoon, as we journeyed over to old Aliso, we noticed four police cars staked out at the foot of the hills. One police officer shouted to us, "Stand back!" We were told that an escaped convict was hiding in the same hills that had been home to our treasured rocks. Angela and I stood dangerously close by as a crossfire of bullets hurled through the air between the police officers and the escaped convict.

Finally, the police overwhelmed the man hiding in the thick bushes. I was stunned when a Black, slender teenage boy emerged from the hills with trembling hands cupped behind his neck. Tears dotted his face as he nervously stumbled towards the police car. His dread-filled eyes conveyed a deep sense of being lost. I understood instantly that he was not a hardened criminal . . . he was a child. He was immediately handcuffed and placed in the back seat of one of the police cars.

**

My mother entered a contest that offered a brand new bike as first prize. She announced that if she won the bike, she would give it to her oldest. When she won and brought it home, she handed it over to my brother Mike and corrected herself from what she had said earlier — she meant her oldest *boy*. I was really hurt and went over to Angela's house for moral support. Angela owned a bike and generously offered to let me use it anytime I wanted. In light of what my mother had done, I was more determined than ever to learn. After a tremendous amount of practice and bruises, I finally mastered the art of bike riding.

I rode behind Angela to the paper factory and literally jumped into the giant paper bin right outside. We carelessly laughed and playfully tossed paper back and forth as we felt it ripping and tearing beneath us.

Lost in our fun one afternoon, I noticed blotches of blue ink trailing down my arms: we were buried in a sea of carbon paper sandwiched between some office forms. It took us days to remove all the ink from our skin.

Our biggest thrill was skateboards. Back in those days, the skateboard itself was made of wood with metal skate wheels nailed to the bottom. In addition to all the other skills I had to develop in order to keep up with Angela, riding a skateboard was one more. Interestingly, I remember many times falling off Angela's bike while learning to ride, and the countless bruised knees as I came crashing down on the cement sidewalks while learning to skate; however, I do not remember a single time that I fell off my skateboard.

Within days, I learned to take corners and hills with ease. The feel of a skateboard was very different than skates. For me it took a lot less effort to balance myself on a skateboard than it did on skates. My skateboard became the wings beneath my feet. Angela and I flew through Aliso Village with a speed and agility that probably put a lot of the boys to shame!

On many Halloweens, Angela mapped out all the stores on Brooklyn Avenue. We canvassed them instead of the homes and lugged a heavy shopping bag brimming with candy all the way home.

As I reached adolescence, Angela's home became mine every Saturday night while her mother went out dancing. Early the following morning Angela and I always tumbled out of bed. She dutifully removed the old, black cast iron pot from its usual resting place and we were on our way.

My face felt cleansed by the brisk, morning air as we headed towards one of the many food stores that dotted First Street. We busily chatted as we waited in the crowded entrance of the only store that specialized in Mexican food. The hot corn tortillas warmed the cool air as they rolled out on a conveyer belt and fell onto a piece of white butcher paper to be freshly wrapped. After an extended wait, Angela held out her pot and a man generously poured *menudo* (a savory soup made from hominy and tripe) into its belly.

Displayed in a glass case, freshly baked *pan dulce* (Mexican sweet bread), intricately decorated with pink patches of sugar, and freshly baked cookies with multicolored speckles added a festive decor to the simple store. The flaky pumpkin turnovers that fell apart to the touch were my favorite. My childhood sweet tooth would not allow me to leave that store until I had a piece of *calavasa* (a Mexican candy with a soft pumpkin center buried inside a hard shell of sugar-sweetened pumpkin).

Angela and I had our priorities set for Saturday evenings: listening to the latest tunes, practicing the newest dance steps (which changed every other week), and chatting about the most interesting of all subjects — boys.

One evening, a sewing needle found its way into Angela's hand. I watched with curiosity as she approached the gas stove, turned on a burner, and immersed the tip of the needle into the flame. Suddenly, she turned and gestured for me to give her my hand. She plucked my finger with the warm needle and then her own. She tightly pressed our fingers together and proudly announced that we were now *blood sisters*.

**

Another child joined Angela's family when she was about twelve — a healthy baby girl. A little over a year later, a boy was born. He suffered from severe retardation and blindness due to a doctor who allowed Angela's mother to be exposed to measles during her prenatal checkups. Angela's mother proudly insisted on keeping her son and raising him herself.

The first school Angela and I attended was Hollenbeck Junior High. It was during our second year at Hollenbeck that I noticed unusual mood swings in Angela. One afternoon I decided to pick her up unannounced. As I quietly approached the entrance to her last class and peeked inside, I saw some students aimlessly wandering around the classroom; others were seated at their desks, laughing and talking. I instantly noticed the naked surface of the teacher's desk in front of the class, a glistening blackboard untouched by chalk, and the shocking realization that no teacher had ever taught in that classroom.

When Angela arose from her desk, she saw me. As she hung her head in shame, she tightly gripped a piece of paper dangling in her hand to position the visible side away from my view — a piece of paper with academic exercises designed for a very young elementary school student instead of someone our age. I ventured to ask why there was no teacher in her classroom.

A mixture of hurt, anger and frustration raged in her voice. "I don't need a teacher to do this stupid baby work!"

Angela would finally succumb to drugs. Perhaps she was trying to numb the painful and stifling reality of falsely being labeled a *slow learner* which resulted in her being denied a high school education. "A mind is a terrible thing to waste!" Through junior high and high school, there was no excuse for the tragic waste of this creative, adventurous and imaginative mind that sparked *my* childhood with so much magic! (Incidentally, Angela later became a high-placed leader in a well-known Los Angeles gang.)

10

Two Little Girls

An artist could not draw a face more placid nor a body that moved with more grace. Sara's smooth, black skin and high cheekbones suggested the face of a model. Her long fingers, like the stems of a rose, would slowly glide across a blank sheet of paper and create the most beautiful drawings I ever saw. Sara designed clothes in her drawings that looked worthy of being displayed in *Vogue.* She was a gifted artist.

I occasionally went home with her after school. The wardrobes she designed for our many paper dolls — dresses, coats, hats and shoes — were far superior to the store-bought clothes. Sara also fashioned living rooms, bedrooms and bathrooms for our paper dolls from old Blue Chip Stamp catalog photographs. She cut out magazine pictures of faraway places . . . we imagined ourselves on vacation, enjoying the sights. Such were the dreams of *two little girls.*

One afternoon, as we were touring Spain, a loud voice interrupted our childhood fantasy. Sara's mother angrily ordered her to immediately come downstairs. Sara was given the task of cleaning the entire kitchen alone while her siblings were allowed to watch television. Tears began to well up in Sara's sunken eyes as she slowly began scrubbing the dirty pots and pans piled up in the kitchen sink.

I picked up a pot and began to wash it. Though not nearly as severe, Sara's mother's treatment of her was a haunting reminder of my foster home experience. I felt a deep sense of sympathy for the sorrow buried in Sara's eyes.

As we were washing the pots and pans, I remembered entering for the first time the creaky, old wooden front door to the small house her mother rented. In the tiny living room, Sara's younger sister and brother sat watching television. The striking contrast in appearance between them and Sara took me completely by surprise: their skin was a light, creamy shade of brown, golden highlights ran through their hair, and Sara's baby brother even had green eyes; only Sara's mother was very dark like her.

I witnessed the treatment of Sara on several occasions and concluded that her darker skin was the reason for the constant, harsh punishments to which her lighter-skinned siblings were never subjected. I do understand that Sara's mother was the product of a world that taught her to feel that way. The tragedy is that this realization did not come soon enough for Sara.

**

Sara and I joined a recreation center near the Pico housing projects. A very light-skinned Black woman named Mrs. Wilson was the director and our instructor. The first thing she taught our class was modern dance. We designed leaves from green construction paper and attached them to our arms and legs. The music directed our movements as Sara and I effortlessly glided across the hardwood gymnasium floor. We were lost for a glorious moment in a beautiful world of movement without thought.

Our next project was drama. Mrs. Wilson decided on the play "Cinderella." All of our names were written on pieces of paper and placed in a glass bowl; the following week, our names were to be drawn by Mrs. Wilson. For the entire week, Sara talked about being Cinderella. I also wanted the part but not the way Sara did. I felt it was extremely important to her and hoped she was chosen.

Sara and I arrived early to the empty gymnasium the following week. Soon, all the other ten-year-olds came trailing in to join us and chatter filled the silent gym. Mrs. Wilson made her entrance with the glass bowl secured in one arm and her usual clipboard in the other. We all waited in anxious anticipation as Mrs. Wilson pulled the first name from the glass bowl for the lead part of Cinderella. The sound of *my* name stunned me. Instinctively, I turned to Sara in anticipation of the hurt welled up in her eyes. Mrs. Wilson proceeded to pick names from the glass bowl.

As Sara heard her name being read for the part of the mean stepmother, her back instantly stiffened. Her eyes widened, begging to be relieved of the flood of tears trapped behind them, but her pride would not allow it. Instead, she suddenly pulled herself up and stormed out of the gymnasium, kicking open the metal double doors to the entrance and loudly slamming them behind her. Her anger and hurt hung heavily in the air as Mrs. Wilson tried to ignore it and continued calling names.

After our class I walked over to Mrs. Wilson and meekly suggested that Sara and I exchange parts. I explained that being Cinderella was more important to Sara than it was to me. Mrs. Wilson roared, "Sara is not running the show around here!"

As I exited the gym, I noticed Sara standing near a fence outside. I approached her and she angrily glared at me. She lashed out with countless insults but I knew her too well to believe them. As our friendship crumbled under the weight of Sara's hurt and pain, my heart cried out in silence.

Mrs. Wilson was not an insensitive person. She had a deep love for children and a sincere commitment to being a participant in the lives of ghetto children. The positive characteristics I have been able to develop within myself are a product of people like Mrs. Wilson touching my life. However, in Sara's case, Mrs. Wilson lacked awareness of her situation at home and the emotional neediness it had created in her. Yes, Sara was pushy at times and demanded a lot of attention; however, she was only demanding what she desperately needed emotionally and could not find at home. She was loudly crying out for help and all the adults around her lacked the insight to respond to her needs.

Sara wanted to feel beautiful in a world that constantly implied that she was ugly. Mrs. Wilson was a figure of authority which made her opinion important to Sara. Mrs. Wilson, like Sara's siblings, was a Black woman with a very fair complexion. This added fuel to the burning pain created in Sara's home. It was a bad combination that deeply impacted Sara's perception of herself and others. The mean stepmother became the mean Sara. In the final conclusion, the person to whom Sara was meanest was herself.

Out of rage and frustration emerged a Sara who became lulled by drugs to calm the violent storms locked within her. The complex web was woven and the spider came to claim its prey.

11

Worlds Apart

Upon the hillside slope a lush, thick blanket of emerald green grass glistened in the bright sunlight. Clean, shiny cars crowded the parking lot at the foot of the hill; backpacks, suitcases, tennis rackets and a swarm of girls emerged. To my amazement, their reddish-blonde hair, blue eyes, and fair skin looked just like mine!

A Black girl named Genie and I were selected by Mrs. Wilson to go to Hollywoodland Camp for one week, paid through a program sponsored by the *Herald Examiner.* Genie and I formed a special friendship as we were the only two ghetto girls in the entire camp.

Genie and I sat like spectators observing a world far from our own. As we watched the camp come alive, one of the counselors motioned to join her and her group. We were all taken to one of the bungalows located far up on the right side of the hill. Metal beds and lockers lined the bare walls inside. Most of the girls treated Genie and me with a pronounced amount of respect —

prompted, we knew, by fear. It hurt our feelings at first but we learned to laugh about it later.

As we quietly put our things away in a locker, a boisterous sound suddenly shattered the silence. A girl came crashing through our bungalow door with her hands firmly planted on her hips; her mother lagged behind, lugging two heavy suitcases. When the mother finally reached the girl's bed, she placed the suitcases on the floor with a notable sigh of relief.

Instantly, the daughter dumped the contents of the suitcases on her bed. She quickly turned to her mother, who was still catching her breath, and ordered her to put her clothes away in the metal locker next to her bed. The mother worked feverishly as she carefully folded each article of clothing and placed it into the locker.

When the mother completed that task, her daughter ordered her to make the bed with very specific instructions to tuck the sheets under the corners of the mattress exactly the way she liked it. The daughter warned that if the sheets were not folded properly at the corners, she would not sleep in that bed.

Genie and I looked at each other in amazement and rolled our eyes. Genie whispered, "Just *one day* in Aliso Village would teach that girl some respect for her mama!"

Hollywoodland Camp was a bewildering experience for me. One evening as I lay in bed, a haunting thought invaded my mind: I suddenly realized that I felt no emotional attachment to my own race. A deep sense of sadness overwhelmed me as my tears soaked a large corner of my pillowcase.

✳✳

I woke up the next morning to the sounds of chirping birds. Later, I went down to the recreation room and made some Indian jewelry. I then wandered out of the room and followed the sound of "Heart And Soul" being played on the piano by a little girl in a large, open room. She continued playing a variety of songs as I listened with much enjoyment.

A Russian Jewish girl was assigned to our bungalow a couple of days after we had arrived. Deep brown eyes timidly peeked out of a mass of coarse, thick black hair. Her long nose and high cheekbones distinctly resembled those of my mother. *She should have been my mother's daughter instead of me*, I thought. It really bothered me that my physical appearance so strikingly contrasted my mother's Russian Jewish features. I was often asked in the sixth grade if I was adopted.

The girl with the boisterous voice, who ordered her mother around on that first day, began picking on the Russian Jewish girl. One afternoon the poor girl, crying hysterically, ran out of our bungalow and decided to go home. Genie and I talked her out of it. We told her that we would take care of the situation.

That evening Genie and I waited far into the night, quietly tiptoed out of bed with flashlights in hand, and slowly made our way over to the boisterous girl's bed. She was sleeping soundly as we gently lifted her blanket, placed our flashlights near her face and, like a tent hovering above us, pulled the blanket over our heads. Her eyes opened and widened with terror as Genie and I used our ghetto image to frighten her. We warned her that if she bothered that Russian Jewish girl again, we would pack her into one of her suitcases and ship her home. That took care of *that* problem — she never bothered that Russian Jewish girl again.

* *

As soon as I began to really feel relaxed and enjoy myself, it was time to go home. I watched as a parade of cars drove up and a flock of parents with waiting arms emerged. As I observed the many fathers kissing their daughters with open affection, I sadly remembered the last time my father had kissed me.

The parking lot quickly thinned out. The girls disappeared into cars until the last one was gone ... I was all alone. I did not know that two camp counselors were still in the recreation room. For a moment, I imagined that my mother was going to abandon me just like my father had done. I burst into tears as the two camp counselors came running out of the recreation center. It came as a total surprise to them that a girl had not been picked up. I heard one of them say, "It is so unusual."

I was finally driven home by the two camp counselors. When they approached Aliso Village, I could see the terror developing in their eyes. They hurriedly let me out of their car in the parking lot and quickly sped away. My time in another world had ended.

12

Guardian Angel

Chicken smothered in a deep red, homemade barbecue sauce, and white corn bread baked in a black iron skillet with butter instantly melting on its steaming hot surface beckoned me to the table. Sandra, the little girl that lived upstairs, was now my friend. We used our corn bread to wipe up every last drop of that savory sauce still clinging to our dinner plates.

I was really looking forward to spending the night at Sandra's house. She and her friends invited me to go to a James Brown concert. When we arrived, crowds of excited Black teenagers suddenly surrounded us. I felt their joy and pride as they instantly snapped to attention when James Brown jumped onto the stage. Like lightning, his feet flew through the air, making little contact with the ground. His voice blared out of loudspeakers as he sang, "Papa's Got a Brand New Bag" and "I Feel Good." The excitement was infectious. I felt free enough to dance and sing along with everyone else. I had a great time.

On another occasion, I remember watching Sandra with great curiosity as she placed a heavy metal comb on top of a hot stove burner. She rubbed what appeared to be Vaseline in her hair. She cautiously picked up the scorching metal comb with a pot holder wrapped around its handle. Gingerly, she lifted the comb up closely to her scalp and slowly pulled it through her hair. Instantly, all the natural curl became straight and limp — a process called "pressing."

I had a habit of writing letters when I was a child. One day Sandra asked me why I wrote letters. I told her that it was easier for me to write about my feelings than talk about them . . . Sandra understood.

A short time later, she decided to draft a letter to her mother. I can still picture her mother's tear-stained face as she read the letter out loud in our apartment to my mother. Sandra expressed her hurt and pain about the stern discipline she received at home. She explained to her mother that hitting her with an extension cord was not necessary in order to teach her respect.

The letter devastated Sandra's mother. She was trying to teach her children right from wrong the same way she was taught. It was almost impossible for her to understand how her method of discipline could be harmful to her children. (Keep in mind that it was Sandra's mother standing behind Sandra with an extension cord the day Sandra confessed to beating me up; it was also Sandra's mother who insisted Sandra tell the truth.)

Perhaps the method Sandra's mother used was wrong, but the principle she taught her daughter was not. I realize now that Sandra understood the concept of self-respect because her mother taught her to value the quality that produces it: honesty.

**

A few years later, Angela and I were walking through the Pico housing projects and a group of unfamiliar Mexican girls marched towards us. The one that appeared to be the leader stepped forward and eyed me with intense hostility. It was a real shock to me in light of the fact that my friends, all Mexican and Black, treated me as though I were one of them and caused me to often forget I was different.

With tremendous malice, the leader referred to me as a "white patty." Fiercely, she challenged me to a fight with her and her cohorts. Instantly, Angela stepped in front of me and sternly warned the girl that she would have to go through her to get to me.

The leader stepped back in complete amazement at the sight of a member of her own race protecting a White person and acted as though she had never witnessed this before. Until that moment, I never gave a lot of thought to how my friendship with Angela appeared to other people. The leader stated a time and place where Angela and I should meet her and her gang. When Angela accepted their challenge to meet them the very next day, I almost passed out.

I could not permit Angela to face these girls alone on my behalf. Angela had a tremendous amount of pride and courage; I did not. Angela was not about to back down from anyone. If she was afraid, I never saw it. I finally worked up enough courage to go with her, surely our last day on this earth. Twelve of them against two of us; knives and razor blades against our bare hands. We did not have a chance of surviving this battle (or so I thought).

When we arrived, it was quiet and unexpectedly deserted. We waited almost an hour; they never showed up. Sandra approached Angela and me a few days later. She informed us that she heard about the gang that was going to jump us. She told us that her friends, who belonged to a gang called "The Bloods," warned these girls not to touch us or they would have "The Bloods" on *their* hands.

I stood completely stunned as Sandra continued talking. In the years to come, I often wondered how Sandra was able to find out so quickly that Angela and I were in trouble. How was she able to move so swiftly in less than twenty-four hours to prevent an incident that could have cost Angela and me our lives? If there are angels walking around on this earth disguised as human beings, Sandra is one of them.

13

Inez

It was a busy morning in my eighth grade homeroom. We met there before classes as an orientation to guide us through the rest of the day. We were told that a new girl would be joining our homeroom who had extensive medical problems which had not allowed her to attend school on a regular basis. In light of this, our class decided to elect her honorary homeroom class president.

We were never given the exact details of her medical problems; I pictured someone hobbling into our classroom, staring out of a window all day. In stark contrast to all of my expectations, a girl with chocolate-brown skin, silky black hair and bright shiny eyes (the perfect picture of health) waltzed into our homeroom and identified herself as Inez. Her appearance was more Polynesian than Mexican. The luminous smile lighting up her face and the warmth glowing in her eyes gave no hint of illness.

Inez was a real mystery to me, so I made it a point to introduce myself and initiate a friendship. Inez was very receptive to my introduction and we soon became friends. I could feel a loneliness that seemed strange to me because I could not imagine anyone disliking Inez. I did not yet understand what it was like to spend most of your childhood in a hospital.

Inez lived in a different world than most ghetto children. Her spirit seemed untainted by the urgent doubts and fears common to most ghetto children. There was an unusual calmness and innocence preserved in her. Her long stays in the hospital had sheltered her from some of the tragic circumstances that shaped the way so many ghetto children saw the world. Inez was different and that difference never ceased to ignite my curiosity.

Inez lived in the Pico housing projects. When we began walking home after school, I had the opportunity to meet and get to know all of her family — Inez was the oldest of seven children. Inez was one of the few children in the ghetto that resided with both of her natural parents. Her family always welcomed me and an abundance of affection always warmed her home.

I never asked Inez about her medical problems. (Perhaps it was because, when you are a child, what you cannot see does not exist for you.) This way of thinking created a veil of normalcy that would one day be abruptly lifted.

**

One afternoon, without warning, I received an urgent and hysterical phone call from one of Inez's sisters. "Inez has been rushed to the hospital! I don't think she's going to make it this time!"

My hand trembled as I stood there in complete disbelief. I tried to assure Inez's sister that Inez was going to be all right, only half believing my own words. I nervously jotted down the name and number of the hospital on a piece of paper.

When I called, I was told that Inez was in intensive care and was unable to take any phone calls. I was advised to call the next day and check on her condition. The next morning I was terrified of the possibility that Inez did not make it. I finally called and was told that she was doing better; I was greatly relieved.

I continued calling, day after day, until I was allowed to talk to Inez. Her voice sounded distant and weak but her spirit was up and slightly cheerful. She even laughed once during the first conversation. I suggested visiting her and she asked me how I would travel there. I told her I would call the Rapid Transit District for instructions.

The first trip was the most difficult. I transferred buses as instructed and arrived on schedule. As I dismounted, I felt lost and disoriented. The ominous buildings seemed to wrap all the way around the corner and into infinity. I felt like a tiny figurine walking through the enormous main entrance of Children's Hospital in Los Angeles.

I walked down the corridor and noticed that there were no beds lining the hallways like in County Hospital. I pushed the elevator button and walked inside . . . only moments now before I would see Inez. I slowly stepped off the elevator and into the hallway. The receptionist's cheerful greeting sharply contrasted the usual blank stare and "What do *you* want?" I always received from County Hospital.

As I approached Inez's room my apprehension grew. I drew closer and noticed that her door was slightly cracked open. I saw Inez struggling with a doctor and several nurses as they held her down and punctured the sole of her foot with a long, thick needle. Inez let out a piercing scream that lodged itself deeply in my soul. She whimpered in agony as the thick needle was slowly removed from her foot.

I rushed back to the reception desk feeling extremely shaken. I asked the nurse if she would announce my arrival to Inez. The nurse returned and instructed me to go right in.

Inez was sitting up in bed. Her infectious smile almost made me forget what I just saw and heard moments earlier. When I hugged her, I could feel her body still quivering from the pain she had just endured. I told Inez that our homeroom missed her. "When is our classroom president coming home?"

She laughed with a measured effort; she was very weak. I made the visit short and told Inez I would return the following week. I visited Inez on a regular basis, about four times a month. During each visit she grew notably stronger and a healthy glow returned to her skin and eyes. She was responding well to her medical treatment. I was relieved and grateful that Inez was still alive.

During my first visit after Inez's return home from the hospital, her father asked me to step into the kitchen. I saw tears trickle down his face. He slowly looked away and softly spoke of the deep appreciation he and his wife wanted to extend to me for spending so much time with Inez in the hospital. I was touched beyond measure by his boundless emotion and overwhelming gratitude. I saw the years of worry outlined on his face from watching his daughter dance on a constant tightrope between life and death.

Inez's childhood was a testimony to courage. Her spirit was a wind passing quickly through this world — a wind stirring up the leaves that would otherwise lie still on the ground. Every time I think about Inez, I realize that we are the leaves on the ground until someone like her comes along and changes our lives forever.

PART IV

Romantic Relationships: How They Are Impacted By The Ghetto

14

My Mother's Shame

Safely secured behind a silver wire fence, a small and modest home sat alone on an abandoned block surrounded by empty dirt lots across the street from Aliso Village. The tiny mani-cured front lawn and meticulously clean porch were in sharp contrast to the row of dreary brick buildings and half-dead lawns across the street. An elderly Hispanic woman often sat alone on the old wooden porch, staring out at the deserted neighborhood and perhaps entertaining the memories of when it had once been brimming with families.

One summer afternoon (the kind in which the warm sun holds the earth closest to its bosom), I saw a bright light flicker in this old woman's life. Her lonely eyes were suddenly aglow as she watched a young man approach. The sun played in his dark brown eyes as they glistened with light. His spirit was like that of a young buck eager to explore the immense forest for the first time. I knew instantly that he was her son. His name was Robert.

Angela, a girl named Virgie, Robert and I became good friends. We girls had never known someone who had graduated from college. Robert would share all of his dreams and exciting plans to travel around the world. He described, with great enthusiasm, all of the countries he was going to visit. Robert mailed postcards addressed to me but written for all three of us to share. I would wait by the mail box for their arrival, careful to conceal them from my mother. (In light of the fact that Robert was twenty-four and I was fourteen, I felt it would be a friendship difficult for my mother to understand.)

The final postcard Robert sent crossed over the line of friendship and ignited feelings of romance. It arrived just as all the others had before it. As I carefully removed it from the mail box with a nail file, I curiously examined the brightly colored photo on the front of the postcard — a beautiful dancing woman, perhaps somewhere in India. I was immediately taken by the festive mood the picture created in me and casually flipped the postcard over to read it before I took it to share with Angela and Virgie.

I was surprised to see that the salutation, unlike all the others, was written only to me. My eyes suddenly moved more cautiously as I read the neatly printed words: "I am developing a strange affection for you." (There was more but I cannot remember the exact words.) I was instantly stunned and flattered that I could attract a person like Robert — a college graduate! I really liked Robert; however, the thought of a romantic relationship never crossed my mind because of the age difference. I automatically assumed that Robert saw me as a fourteen-year-old girl . . . not a woman.

Suddenly I began to conjure up images of Robert and me floating away into the sunset, like two lovers destined to be united in spite of the years that divided them. I also entertained the fanciful idea of skipping past my teens and instantaneously leaping into adulthood . . . it was a glorious dream!

✳ ✳

A twinge of embarrassment rippled through me when I first saw Robert upon his return. Unusually quiet, the prospect of instant adulthood began to create a tinge of anxiety in me. I stood there grappling with my own uncertain feelings as Angela chatted on, completely unaware of the final postcard.

Perhaps she noticed the tension that existed between Robert and me as she posed her unexpected question, "What would you do if you were engaged to Kathy?"

As I gasped with complete surprise, Robert instantly darted a knowing smile in my direction. "I wouldn't complain."

While we were visiting Robert at his mother's house one evening, Angela and Virgie left early; Robert and I were alone for the first time. We sat in the living room and talked for awhile. "You have a very mature mind for your age," Robert remarked.

I was deeply flattered by such a compliment coming from a college graduate and shyly whispered, "Thank you."

Midway through the conversation the subject of my mother arose. Threads of anxiety immediately formed hard knots in my stomach as Robert asked, "Can I meet your mother?"

"Sure," I nervously responded, completely uncertain of my ability to fulfill his request.

That evening, as I felt the pressure mounting, I cautiously approached my mother. She was standing in the tiny kitchen in front of the stove, slowly stirring some spaghetti sauce with a wooden spoon.

I talked briefly about Robert, emphasizing that he was a college graduate, but careful not to mention the postcards. My mother busily stirred her sauce and casually listened. When the long-awaited question finally formed on my lips, "Robert wants to meet you," the sounds resonated in her ears. My mother was suddenly yanked from her calm mood as she flipped the wooden spoon out of the deep, red sauce, instantly spattering the wall. An overwhelming dread consumed her and she trembled with intense fear.

Puzzled and confused by her reaction, I frantically attempted to calm her down. When she pleaded through her tears, "Please don't bring him here because he will not approve of me," her words — like poison darts — struck me directly in the heart . . . the shame that once belonged only to my mother now belonged to me.

I had to end that relationship, not only because of what my mother felt, but because of what I now felt about myself. I instinctively knew that if I wanted to keep Robert, I would be required to share my mother's (and now my own) pain and humiliation with him. I was not emotionally prepared to do that at fourteen. I discontinued visiting Robert without an explanation. A short time later, I had my tonsils removed and Robert paid me an unexpected visit in the hospital. I was grateful that the operation left me temporarily unable to speak.

One afternoon as I was walking alone, I ran into Robert. I was wearing a mini skirt which all of my friends wore during those days. The anger bristled in his voice as he demanded to know why I was wearing such a short skirt. I knew his anger had nothing to do with the length of my skirt; he was angry because I left him emotionally hanging without an explanation. I did not know how to end our relationship in a mature way. That was the last time I ever saw Robert.

15

The Gentle Artist

When Angela and I heard music through the windows of the old Dolores Mission Catholic school auditorium, our curiosity was aroused. Our eyes lit up and our thoughts registered in unison. We slowly approached the double doors that led into the gymnasium. Two nuns protectively guarded the entrance as we nervously slipped past their stern demeanors and cautious glances.

Teenage boys and girls lined opposite sides of the room. Some of them were gathered around a large refreshment table covered with a variety of food and soft drinks. Suddenly, a new round of live music broke the nervous silence as awkward teenage boys began asking girls to dance.

* *

I felt his glance as the outline of his face emerged from the darkness of the dimly lit room. He was very tall and angular. A hint of his emotions peeked through the parted curtain in his eyes. His

71

approach was reserved as he studied my eyes, facial expressions and physical demeanor. I turned to smile at him and broke his concentration. The serious lines in his face softened into a smile and our relationship began.

Armando and I spent many evenings attending those weekly Catholic high school dances. I can still see the protective eyes of the nuns meticulously examining the distance at which the boys held the girls during the slow dances. Armando attended a Catholic high school and was unaware of some of the things going on around him in the housing projects in which he lived. I was touched by his innocence which endeared him to me even more.

Armando was the oldest of seven children — one of the few families in the Pico housing projects still residing with both natural parents: a proud and hard-working father and a warm, nurturing mother.

Armando was an excellent student and a gifted artist. I spent hours watching him work magic with his charcoal drawing pencils as he etched the gentle face of the mother of Christ. He would shape and form the eyes with the same patience and care they were intended to reflect. With paint, he gave flesh to the face and wove golden hues through the long, dark brown hair. We were windows to one another as our eyes locked and painted our thoughts and feelings without words.

At this point in the relationship, Armando declared to his friends that we were "going around" (going steady). I felt so proud when he presented me with his class ring. Suddenly my joy was overshadowed by a heavy cloud of anxiety as I remembered my mother. *Armando is going to want to meet her,* I nervously thought. I promised myself that I would never make that mistake again: I will devise a plan that will keep Armando and my mother forever apart.

✳ ✳

One warm evening, I cuddled up next to Armando. While enjoying the security of his arms, I falsely described my mother as very confident and strict rather than an alcoholic who felt intensely inferior to other people. Armando accepted my description without reservation. I felt guilty for painting a picture that deviated so far from the truth; ashamed because it was the first time I had ever lied to someone who completely trusted me; angry because my mother's problems had placed me in this position; afraid because I knew that I was building a house of cards.

During the course of my one-year relationship with Armando, his family was suffering a deep financial strain. In their attempt to finance three children in Catholic high schools and four in Catholic elementary schools, they were finally overwhelmed by the burden. Two of Armando's sisters, closest to him in age, suddenly found themselves thrust into the academic dumping grounds of Roosevelt High School. There was a softness in Armando's sisters that I rarely saw in girls attending public school — that was about to change.

One evening, Armando's facial features stiffened with worry as his eyes reached out in agony for my support. Looking away from me, he echoed disbelief and said, "My sister is *pregnant!*"

For a moment I was quiet as I frantically searched for the right words to comfort him. His deep hurt hung over the room. "The father of that baby will never, *ever* step foot in my house!" I knew instinctively that the only thing I could do was listen. Armando's honest display of genuine emotions told me that he knew I loved him from my soul and he trusted me. I felt sick about the lie upon which our relationship was built.

* *

A short time later, Armando's other sister (the one who was a year younger than the pregnant one) was sitting on the stairs in their apartment surrounded by a small crowd of friends. As I was sitting in the living room nearby waiting for Armando to come downstairs, I could hear their conversation. Suddenly a rash of off-color jokes erupted, followed by loud bursts of laughter. It was not until I heard Armando's sister's voice above the chatter that I became deeply shaken. As if by metamorphosis, bitterness had completely transformed her voice.

"I have class up my ass!" Again the tiny crowd roared with laughter immediately following her self-deprecating comment.

That very same evening, as I walked through my front door, my mother confronted me about Armando. (Sandra's mother had seen me with him and had reported it to her.) My initial fear instantly turned into anger as I realized the immense power my mother had over my relationships and my life. As she ordered me to discontinue seeing Armando, I ran into my bedroom and slammed the poorly measured door, lodging it tightly into its door frame. *How apropos*, I angrily thought: in my attempt to squeeze my life into the framework of my mother's problems, I was tightly stuck like that misfitted door.

I could not bring myself to just "drop" Armando, as my mother bluntly put it. Armando and I were far more than casual friends ending an impersonal relationship. I needed a plan that would make breaking up Armando's idea. Then I could bear the hurt of our break up and Armando would be spared the knowledge that our entire relationship was built upon a lie.

I decided to join Angela in ditching (cutting) school, knowing full well that Armando's sister — the one who had made the self-deprecating remark — occasionally ditched with Angela.

Angela once explained to me that the reason she ditched school was because she felt she would not be missed. When I asked her what she meant, she sarcastically remarked, "How can a teacher who is not even there miss you?" The hurt in her eyes said far more than the sting of her words.

My reason for doing this was that if Armando discovered that I had ditched school with his sister, he would hold me responsible for being a bad influence on her. That would be grounds for him to break up our relationship and put him in the position to reject me. The hurt would be mine instead of his. I had no idea of the complicated mess I was about to create and the profound sadness that would result.

✳ ✳

Life felt like an obstacle course to me: dodging stray bullets, angry gang members, drug-infested breezeways, or personal relationships. I was always and forever creating mental tactics as I constantly made the treacherous trek over the numerous mine fields of deadly danger and gut-wrenching pain that seemed to define the reality of my life.

Upon carrying out my carefully devised plan, I went to visit Armando to purposely end our relationship with Armando's pride still intact and keep the truth about my mother forever hidden. As I casually passed through the back door leading to the kitchen, Armando was standing in front of a breadboard making a sandwich. The moment he saw me, he dropped what he was doing and grabbed me by the arm. He pulled me into the living room and onto the sofa. "Did you ditch school with my sister?"

"Yes," I whispered as I glanced up at him with hesitation. For some reason, I expected anger and instant rejection instead of the deep hurt and sad betrayal I found in his eyes.

"I cannot believe that *you*, of *all* people, could do this." His disappointment cut deeply into my heart.

I would see Armando one last time. He had purchased a used car and asked Angela to arrange a meeting to which I reluctantly agreed. In the small, dark space of his car, I reached inside for the right words to fill up the giant space between us; none were forthcoming. I painfully realized that I shattered the trust that once made our silent moments magically alive. Words that were once unnecessary were now mandatory as Armando and I sat there in silent anticipation.

It did not matter why I had broken the trust that once existed between us. It was not important that I did it for what I felt was a justified reason. The sadness still overwhelmed me as I sat there and realized that it was gone.

16

The Teenage Fair

The wall had thickened. I routinely avoided every glance that came my way. My shredded emotions and distraught frame of mind could no longer perform the juggling act necessary for me to conduct a relationship with anyone.

Perhaps the warm glow in his eyes or the broad, genuine smile cast upon his face tempted me. A tiny spark of excitement ignited as a young man made his approach and casually introduced himself as "Richard." With a natural ease, he announced that he was a Garfield High School student. Toward the end of our short chat, he insisted on walking me home; out of fear, I immediately declined his offer.

Several afternoons later, I was surprised to see Richard appear at the gate leading out of Roosevelt. His persistence prompted my respect and I went against my better judgment. I reluctantly agreed to allow him to walk me home.

The green, grassy hills of Hollenbeck Park made the perfect backdrop for our pleasant conversation as we slowly strolled along the cement sidewalks that bordered it. The calmness in Richard's voice lulled me, causing me to let down my guard until we reached Aliso Village. Richard suddenly remarked, barely able to contain his shock, "You actually *live* here?"

"Yes!"

Instantly he glanced away with downcast eyes. "I didn't mean it that way."

"Oh sure," I sarcastically recoiled. Richard followed my comment with a request to again walk me home another day. Not believing that he was sincere, I agreed. I figured I would never see him again and it was probably better that way.

One afternoon the following week, I was truly stunned to see Richard standing at the gate with a genuine look of anticipation beaming in his face. (Outside of my flag girl uniform, I was not the sexy looking type. Most of the time I hardly wore any makeup; I lived in the squalid conditions of Aliso Village; I was deeply withdrawn emotionally and extremely guarded.) It was very difficult to understand what prompted Richard's continued interest . . . it equally intrigued me.

During this walk home, Richard invited me to go with him to the Teenage Fair. A loud voice inside of me screamed *No!* as my head quietly nodded yes.

**

The smell of hot, buttered popcorn and freshly made cotton candy mingled in the open air. The brightly colored rides and busy game stands created a festive atmosphere filled with the promise of fun. The infectious joy etched on so many faces encouraged me to relax a little and let down my nervous guard.

Outwardly, I attempted to imitate the smiles and jovial expressions exuding on the faces around me. I pushed my true feelings a short distance away as I grappled with an internal ocean of anxiety spilling into my eyes. I hated those tiny windows that always threatened to expose me.

I felt Richard's eyes intently fixed on me as he said with grave concern, "There is so much sadness in your eyes."

I could feel my heart rapidly pounding like a small, frightened animal caught in an invisible trap it could not see or touch. I glanced downward, feeling terribly naked and vulnerable. There was nowhere to hide the tangled web of chaos reflected on the wet and glossy surface of my eyes. I let Richard's comment and our budding friendship dangle in the air as I continued to emotionally fade away.

Part V

Their Constant Exposure To Death: Shaping Their Perception Of Life

17

Cause of Death

Sharp screams ripped through the air. I dashed through the front door of an Aliso apartment and found a very young pregnant Black woman in agonizing pain. She tightly clutched the refrigerator door handle for support and slowly slid onto the kitchen floor. Suddenly, a neighbor (also a Black woman) rushed into the apartment and assisted the pregnant woman over to the couch.

A little boy emerged from one of the bedrooms and hesitantly approached his expectant mother, now sprawled out across the sofa and whimpering in pain. His eyes widened with fear as he cautiously examined his mother's body. His small arms protectively embraced her as he buried his head against the softness of her bosom.

An ambulance was summoned; many more neighbors began to crowd in and around the doorway of the tiny apartment. The pregnant mother faded in and out of consciousness, crying and screaming in anguish. All her strength was spent and she disappeared into another restless sleep.

One hour passed . . . two hours passed. No ambulance arrived. Now delirious with pain, her sharp cries were followed with mumbled words. The neighbor who had called the ambulance continued to wet a washcloth with cool water and gently place it on the expectant mother's feverish forehead.

The son clung to his mother's body. The young mother's torment reached its climax as she cried out one last time. Moments later, death erased all pain from her face as she and her unborn child quietly passed away.

It took another half hour before an ambulance finally arrived. The pregnant woman was hurriedly placed onto a stretcher and hauled away as her little son screamed out in protest. There was a man standing next to me, writing something on a form. I glanced over and read, "Cause of death due to complications of pregnancy."

18

Many Children Died There

One afternoon, as I pushed open the front door, my mother was angrily ranting on the phone about a little Black boy that had just been run over by a car. "He was just crossing that damn street without a crosswalk or traffic light. He was knocked over like a piece of cardboard by one of those cars coming off the bridge at 55 miles per hour. How many little children are going to have to die before someone *finally* puts a crosswalk or traffic light on that damn intersection?"

A crosswalk and underground tunnel were provided on one side of First Street to protect the safety of the children that walked to and from Utah Elementary School every day. However, on the opposite side of First Street where another intersection existed, no crosswalk or light was provided. Fast-moving cars would come down from a bridge on First Street and reach the first intersection with nothing to stop or even slow them down.

The children were supposed to use the side of the street with the crosswalk and light. There were many children that lived closer to the other side of First Street and did not understand the danger. Some of them decided to use the street without the crosswalk or light. Drivers coming off the bridge had no warning that a child might decide to walk or even dart out across the street.

Some time later, after the death of the little boy in this story, a crosswalk was finally put in. I do not really know who or what motivated that action, but the fact that it took the death of many small children speaks for itself.

I thought for many years about the lesson to be learned from that incident. As I grew older, I came to understand that if this child had lived in a middle-class neighborhood and was killed because of a missing crosswalk or traffic light, the people in that community would have sued the county or city in which they lived for neglect and easily won their case.

The most distressing thing about this incident was that it revealed what motivates most people who are in positions of authority to take action that affects the welfare and safety of ghetto children. It is not a genuine concern for the well-being of these children but rather a fear of retribution.

I would like to dedicate this chapter to all those children who unnecessarily lost their lives. If this motivates the writing of a new law that not only seeks in words but provides in action a mandatory level of safety equivalent to that outside the ghetto, none of those children will have died in vain.

19

The Black Wreath

One afternoon, as I was walking through old Aliso, a loud explosion rattled the ground beneath me. Startled and confused, I ran into a breezeway thinking that it was an earthquake. Moments later, when the ground was perfectly still, I realized that it was an explosion.

I followed the smell of smoke. As it grew stronger, I knew I was moving closer to the source. I turned the corner and saw a crowd of people who stood before the two-story apartment that was completely ablaze. One of the upstairs bedroom window panes exploded and red hot flames of fire spewed forth. Terror engulfed me as I heard the screams of very young children and an infant held hostage inside.

My eyes raced in all directions, hoping to see a fire truck; all I saw were people screaming and crying, "Oh Lord, please don't let them *babies* die!"

The screams grew louder as the sinister heat continued to rip through the apartment. I heard one Black man yell, "Where is that damn fire truck?" and another man angrily shout, "Those kids gonna be dead and gone up to heaven before that damn fire truck gets its tail here!"

Like the explosions that ripped the window panes from their frames, the searing screams of these small children ripped at the hearts of everyone there. The infant continued to wail and shriek as it made its plea for relief. The ominous blanket of fire completely smothered its last sounds as the crowds stood helpless.

The piercing outbursts of the remaining children continued. In desperation, one of the them tried to move towards the window and screamed, "*Mama!*" The body became engulfed in flames and fell to the floor.

The remaining child, horrified at watching the fate of its siblings, screeched with uncontrollable terror. Suddenly, the floor beneath the child surrendered to the heat of the fire and collapsed, killing the child instantly.

A short time later a long, red truck drove up to the skeleton of the apartment and the fire was extinguished. An ambulance finally arrived. With looks of horror etched upon their faces, the paramedics hurriedly removed the remains of the small children and infant in plastic bags. The mother's body was discovered in the living room on the first floor of the apartment and was removed with her children. Large boards were nailed over the shattered windows and severely charred front door.

Some of the people who lived in old Aliso hung a black wreath on the board over the front door as a memorial to the children and mother who lost their lives that day.

20

It Never Happened

It was July 6, 1966 ... an early summer evening with the sun dimly lit in the sky. My ten-year-old sister Pat was awkwardly practicing on her skates. Both my sisters had gone to Sears earlier that day. They were so excited when they returned because my mother had put some school dresses on lay away for them.

A woman nicknamed "Chicken Head" resided across the street from where we lived. Some of the neighborhood kids had assigned her that name because her hair sparsely covered her head, giving her the appearance of a chicken. Chicken Head always seemed angry and easily irritated. She would not allow her children to play with the other children in the neighborhood. The situation created a lot of jealousy.

A woman named Dorothy and Chicken Head were constantly arguing. There were numerous bottle fights where the sudden noise of shattered glass erupted, bringing large numbers of people out on their balconies.

This day was no different. My sister knew how the fight started ... she was there. Dorothy's son was riding his bicycle; Chicken Head's kids were playing jump rope. Dorothy's son decided he would ride his bike through the jump rope just to be mean. As his bike came in contact with the jump rope, he fell off. He was caught by the neck with the rope, leaving burns on his skin. He rushed home to tell his mother that Chicken Head's kids attempted to choke him with a rope.

My sister and her friend looked on in terror as the angry mother walked past them, placing a knife in the belt of her shorts and covering it with her blouse. She picked up a pipe and continued to approach Chicken Head who was now waiting for her in the center of our front lawn.

Dorothy yelled, "Your children choked my child with a rope and I want you to let my child choke your children back!"

Chicken Head immediately sent her children upstairs as she refused Dorothy's request. A multitude of people began to fill the balconies as the argument grew louder. My sister saw Chicken Head pull out what at first appeared to be only a cap gun. (At least she hoped it was.) Moments later, when she pointed the gun at Dorothy's face and fired it, the bullet penetrated Dorothy's jugular vein. The deep, red blood spurted all over her limp body which had collapsed on the ground.

Paralyzed with fear and disbelief, my sister stood there unable to move. Finally, she skated away. She went the long way around our building and, without removing her skates, trekked up the back grated metal stairs with much difficulty. She was still wearing her skates as she entered our apartment.

My mother asked, "What's wrong?"

"Dorothy's been shot!"

"What are you talking about?"

Pat asked, "Didn't you hear the gun shots?"

"I thought they were old fire works." (It was July 6th.)

"No, mom. They *shot* her." My sister ran over to the front window and peered out at the body still sprawled out on our lawn. Dorothy's bloodied face was buried in a soft patch of crimson mud where grass had long since ceased to grow. Before Dorothy fell, she intently glanced over at her son who had falsely accused the children of choking him. He was the last person she would see before she died.

My mother rushed downstairs to try and help the woman dying on our front lawn — she was going to turn her head around so she would not choke on her blood. Some people began to shout at my mother to leave the woman alone and not touch her; other people, who also wanted to help, remained silent out of fear.

My sister had a difficult time understanding why these people objected to my mother helping Dorothy. A deep sense of sadness outlined my mother's face as she came back upstairs. She had always taught us to greatly value life. I guess it hurt her immensely to see this person die and do nothing to try and prevent it.

In our apartment, my sister continued looking out the window. "Mom, why are some people laughing?" (There were actually a few people standing over the body, laughing and making jokes, while others were filled with grief and tears.)

My mother motioned for my sister to come away from the window and asked her, "Why didn't you walk away? I always told you when you see trouble or a fight, to walk away. Why did you just *stand* there? Do you realize you could have been hit?"

"I don't know, mom."

✳ ✳

The police finally showed up. Someone informed them that my sister had been the closest eye witness to the murder. Two police officers loudly knocked on our front door. When my mother opened it, they forcefully pushed their way through and immediately demanded to know which daughter had witnessed the murder. My mother reluctantly pointed to Pat.

The stony expressions on their faces struck a chill in me as they callously flung their barrage of questions at this frightened ten-year-old girl. Pat could barely contain her terror as she mumbled a few answers and slowly stepped behind my mother, physically hiding from them. My mother pleaded with the police officers to end the questioning and exempt my little sister from being called to act as an eye witness to a murder. "She is just a *little girl!*"

Without any regard for my mother's plea, their relentless interrogation continued. A rage swelled within me as I watched my little sister tightly cling to the back of my mother's apron, too terrified to hear — much less answer — one more question.

My mother was harshly warned that a subpoena could be obtained that would force my little sister to answer their questions and serve as an eye witness if she did not cooperate. When the police officers finally left, my mother's hunched shoulders and long face communicated her deep sense of defeat.

"Mom, what am I going to do? They are going to make me a *witness!*" In my sister's mind, Chicken Head was a killer. My sister feared that Chicken Head would come and get her once Chicken Head learned that she was going to be the eye witness.

To put her mind at ease, my mother called a girlfriend who lived on the other side of the village. She talked to her mother and asked if my sister could stay there for a few days. The mother agreed. My sister was so happy to be there and finally feel safe. She really enjoyed herself; it took her mind off the murder and being an eye witness.

Chicken Head called our upstairs neighbor for advice. Our neighbor advised her to turn herself in to the police . . . she did. Shortly after that, my mother informed my sister that it was all right to come home.

Pat was still required to serve as an eye witness in court. My mother accompanied her on the day of the trial. Our upstairs neighbor arranged it so that one of her friends that did not reside in Aliso would drive my sister and mother to court.

My sister was assigned to an attorney who specialized in working with children. His sensitivity to her feelings instilled a new-found confidence. "We don't want to hear anyone else's story." He questioned her knowledge of the difference between the truth and a lie and gently explained, "I want you to just say what you remember. It doesn't matter what people told you, or what you heard, or what you *think* might have happened. Say only what you saw with your own eyes and just be honest. If you really don't remember something, don't worry about it. Say, 'I don't remember.' If you really didn't see something, say you didn't see it." My sister agreed.

When Pat went on the trial stand, she was terrified to look at Chicken Head who was seated directly in front of her during the entire testimony. She told the truth exactly as she remembered it. The key factor in the case hinged on the question, "Did Dorothy lift up the pipe before Chicken Head pulled out her gun?"

My sister answered, "I don't know, because I was talking to my friend. When I looked up I saw Chicken Head — Dorothy was to my side. So I really didn't see what she did."

Several days later my sister asked my mother, "What happened to Chicken Head?"

"They let her go free."

Pat's eyes widened with surprise. "Why? She *murdered* somebody!" In the mind of my ten-year-old sister, the concept of self-defense justifying an act of murder fell far outside the range of her comprehension.

"Well, it turns out that Dorothy had a long criminal record and was a fugitive from the law. She had thrown acid on a sheriff and burned out one of his eyes. They had been looking for her. She had a very violent past." Usually, when she had a fight with Chicken Head, she was the instigator. Perhaps due to all the facts presented to the jury, they finally found Chicken Head innocent because of self-defense.

My sister was kind of a short-lived celebrity in Aliso Village. Kids thought it was a big deal that she had gone to court. Dorothy's children paid the highest price ... all of them were devastated. Shortly after Dorothy's murder, her two-year-old son was found wandering aimlessly through Aliso Village asking, "Where's mama?"

✳ ✳

Many years later, my sister earned a scholarship to the University of Southern California (USC). She had since put the incident behind her. My sister had a college roommate named Maybell. She was seventeen and a gifted student.

As their friendship deepened, Maybell and Pat began to share their past experiences. During one of their conversations, my sister shared her feelings about being only ten years old and an eye witness to a murder, being threatened by police officers to serve in court, and actually serving as an eye witness on the trial stand.

She relived the moment when she peered out the window and watched the bloodied woman spread across our lawn. My sister suddenly felt the gravity of her experience pulling her back to the painful memories that lingered in her mind. She could still see some of the people standing over the body actually laughing, while others remained silent out of fear. Maybell was just as intrigued as she was shocked by my sister's story. She found the nickname Chicken Head very colorful and interesting.

As time moved on, my sister was having difficulty mastering the art of writing, required in almost all of her college classes. In spite of her standing as an honor student at Roosevelt, she was never formally taught simple English grammar — a natural consequence of being educated in ghetto high schools.

She attempted to write about other people because she did not see her ghetto experiences having any positive value. She was asked to write about subjects far outside the realm of her experiences, such as abortion.

One day she was specifically asked to write about one of her own childhood experiences. This request created a real dilemma and she decided to share her feelings with Maybell.

"What am I going to write? I have nothing interesting to write about. I've never *been* anywhere . . . I never *do* anything. What am I going to write about?"

"I think you ought to write about Chicken Head."

Genuinely shocked, my sister asked, "Are you serious? Why?"

"Because it has all the makings of a good story: characters, action, climax and intrigue . . . it has everything. Use the name Chicken Head and describe her. Say what it was like. Really explain and get into it."

Pat began working and Maybell proofread. My sister rewrote it several times; Maybell proofread it each time. Finally Maybell said,

"I like this. This is good . . . it's a good piece of work. Now turn it in. I think your teacher will be pleased."

The afternoon the paper was to be returned, my sister sat in her class anxiously waiting to find out how she did. *Did I write it well?* she silently asked herself. *Did I express my feelings and describe my perceptions vividly?* she wondered. She was absolutely sure of one thing: it took a tremendous amount of strength to open up such a painful wound buried deeply in her heart and pour it out on a piece of paper. This was not just a story: this was a piece of her soul — the soul of a ghetto child.

The teaching assistant hurriedly began passing out the papers. My sister waited with acute anticipation as each paper was handed to someone else. As the stack of papers was reduced to one last sheet, my sister suddenly realized it was hers.

She slowly approached my sister's desk, carefully avoiding any eye contact. She held out the paper with a trembling arm and angrily asserted, *"It never happened!"*

Shocked and humiliated right down to the core of her soul, my sister emotionally retreated for a moment. When she gained hold of herself, she looked up at this woman standing there with accusatory eyes. *I will not be discounted,* she thought.

My sister picked up her paper and purposely forced eye contact. In a calm and self-composed manner, she announced, "This is my life. This happened. It will not be denied." As Pat exited the classroom, she turned to the woman one last time with indignation burning in her eyes. *"It did happen!"*

PART VI

Unspoken Courage: Their Silent Strength

21

A Silent Code of Honor

The sun glistened upon the golden-blond hair of a college-aged girl playing guitar on an Aliso Village lawn. Slowly, small children sat near her and formed a complete circle around her. Her pale blue eyes were soft with emotion. She sang to the children's widened eyes, filled with enchantment and curiosity at the sight of this unusual creature. As I drew nearer to the gentle melodies sweetly flowing through the air, I saw two Black teenage boys briskly walking towards me: trouble.

The two boys approached the young woman on the lawn and angrily ordered her to get up. Each of them grabbed one of her arms and abruptly escorted her out of Aliso Village. As they brushed past me, darting deadly threats at the young girl, they took no notice of my strikingly similar physical features: my golden-blond hair, gray-blue eyes, and fair skin. They yelled at the girl, "No White people allowed in Aliso Village. Ya hear, girl?"

I mounted the stairs to my apartment feeling thoroughly confused. I approached the bathroom mirror and stared into it. The situation was incomprehensible to my young mind: why did they hate *her* for being White but not *me*? Why had the Black teenage boys in the neighborhood bought me ice cream along with the other kids when I was younger? Why did they occasionally play games with me and the other kids? (I often thought of them as big brothers.) It really hurt my feelings to think that they hated the color of my skin. I cried deep down inside.

As this experience grew more distant, I learned to understand that the people in Aliso Village had developed a system that protected my family. They understood that we were trapped there just like they were. In response to our dilemma, they developed a silent code of honor.

22

Just Say No

As I glanced over at his face, barely visible behind the bars of the hospital bed, all I could see was a large puffy mass of tissue covered with bloody slashes. His eyes were swollen shut and disappeared into his face; his arms, hands and fingers were completely buried in bandages.

I was at County Hospital with my mother for her routine iron shots to treat her pernicious anemia.

A middle-aged Mexican man stood at the foot of his son's bed wearing a red plaid flannel shirt and dusty jeans. His badly worn hands tightly clutched one of the metal bars adjacent to the bed. His widened eyes were transfixed upon the hauntingly still body that lay before him. The whole world seemed to rest upon his shoulders. He examined his son; total disbelief deeply etched its way into the grooves of his face.

A doctor finally approached him. "My son a *good* boy!" he explained in newly learned English. "He no want to join gang! That why they *do* this to him! They cut with razor blades," he lamented. His face fell into his hands and he broke into uncontrollable sobs.

His emotional outburst deeply moved me. For the first time, I began to realize the horrible price exacted from parents who are forced to watch their children suffer and die.

✶ ✶

I respect what Mrs. Reagan's "Just Say No" program sought to accomplish. However, as you travel down the socioeconomic ladder of society, the price you pay to "Just Say No" dramatically increases. It becomes clear that the term "Growing Up Against The Odds" means something more than just having less money — it also means having less choices.

Because ghetto incidents such as this are so commonly ignored by the media, let this chapter be the pin awarded to this young man for his courage as seen through the eyes of a young girl.

23

Pushed to the Limit

Several feet were pounding in unison to the repetitious beat loudly vibrating on our bedroom ceiling. The melodic earthquake continued to ring through our ears and break our sleep every Sunday night. The brand new, bright and shiny cars that lined the otherwise bare parking lots of Aliso Village Saturday and Sunday nights were a common sight. Loud and roaring laughter pierced through the brick walls of our tiny apartment as young men and women ran up and down the outside stairs.

One Sunday evening, long after midnight, my mother reached her limit. We needed to get up early in the morning for school. She decided to do something our neighbors were afraid to do: call the police. She hesitated to give her real name, but the police department insisted her name would be kept confidential and promised to investigate the situation upstairs. Reluctantly, my mother gave her real name and address, and the address of the all-night party in progress.

About three in the morning, two policemen knocked on our door. In full view of the men and women still hanging all over the stairs, one policeman loudly announced that he was responding to my mother's complaint against her upstairs neighbors.

My mother immediately asked the two officers to step inside our apartment. She attempted to explain that she only gave her real name because the police department promised to keep her identity confidential. She pointed out that their loud announcement of her complaint against her neighbors could jeopardize the safety of her children and herself.

I heard one of the police officers deride my mother for reporting a crime: "This is *not* Beverly Hills!"

A quiet rage burrowed deep within me. That towering policeman in my tiny living room was reduced, by his own words, to a coward hidden behind a dark blue uniform with a worthless piece of tin pinned to his chest. His blatant mockery of justice would forever be imprinted in my mind and heart.

Moments after the police left, the pimp who lived upstairs called out to my mother from our front lawn. "Get your ass down here, 'cause I gonna kick it good!"

Maybe it was a culmination of all the frustrations that she was forced to endure in Aliso Village; perhaps she was pushed to her limit and her fear finally gave way to rage. She marched to the front door and flung it wide open. As she stormed onto the porch, the pimp looked up at her with complete dismay.

Without hesitation, my mother yelled loudly enough for all of Aliso Village to hear: "You want to kick my ass, you coward pimp? *Here I am!*" My mother approached the stairs and screamed, "You just touch me and I will throw *your* ass right down these stairs!"

The men and women hanging all over the stairs suddenly became silent. They could have ganged up on my mother and easily beaten the daylights out of her, but they decided to end the party instead. The pimp downstairs quietly disappeared under the breezeway.

* *

I learned something very fundamental about people that evening: all people — including pimps and prostitutes — respect courage. There is something deep down inside of us all that renders our hearts naked and reminds us that we are connected when we witness human courage. It lifts us up in spirit, individually and collectively, in spite of all the circumstances that pull us down.

24

The Blind Leading the Blind

She was like a terrified animal caught in an iron trap, screaming out in agony for help. My stomach always twisted and turned into a tight knot whenever I witnessed one of my mother's fits of rage.

One afternoon, as our mother threw food and smashed dishes against the walls of our tiny apartment, a new social worker paid us an unannounced visit. Her unexpected knock instantly jolted my mother back to reality; there was no time for my mother to clean up the mess. As the social worker made her way through the door and inside the apartment, she purposely avoided looking at the food dripping down the walls and the broken pieces of dishes strewn across the floor. She did not once dare to look at, much less question why, my youngest sister huddled in the corner of the living room, still too frightened to move.

The social worker asked my mother a long list of questions, none of them relating to the disturbing condition of our apartment. It was obvious to me (maybe because I was a child) that this social worker was too afraid to be honest with herself about the condition of our lives. She selectively chose her questions so that they never touched upon reality. Her eyes only traveled within a very restricted perimeter inside our tiny apartment, and carefully avoided seeing the complete and very disturbing picture.

✳✳

As a child I felt that social workers were not there to help me. They were there to ignore and pretend that my mother's problems, and therefore my problems, did not really exist.

One day, I met a social worker who I believed was different than most. She did not hide her eyes when she entered our apartment and did something no other social worker had ever done: she befriended me. I think it is probably every ghetto child's dream to discover some magical person that will rescue them from the horribly painful daily reality they must face.

She invited me during one of her social worker visits to go home with her; I accepted eagerly. The wall-to-wall carpeting felt warm and comforting as I entered her apartment; the soft, over-sized sofa and printed pillows hugged my body.

"Why did your mother choose to live in that ghetto instead of accepting financial assistance from your grandfather?" she blurted out.

I remember being very surprised that she knew about that, and reluctantly and softly answered, "I don't know."

"Do you realize how many people are on welfare who *really* need financial aid and have no grandfather to support them?"

I remained silent, mostly out of shock. A wave of undeserving shame, which should have never belonged to me as it was not my decision to make, snarled my emotions.

The greatest surprise came when she explained that my Black and Mexican friends *belonged* in the ghetto, and that because I was White, all I had to do was just get up and *leave.* In spite of the fact that I was a teenager, I clearly understood that this woman had absolutely no comprehension of the world in which I lived and the people who lived in that world with me.

I realized that this social worker saw me as *she* lived, not as *I* lived. In her mind, my white skin erased the father that abandoned me, the alcoholic mother that shaped the sorry self-perception I developed, the foster home that abused me, the nervous breakdown that resulted from that abuse, the two men that sexually molested me, the police department that treated it like a joke, the junior high and high school systems that failed to educate me, and all the other negative experiences in between. Only a very blind person could believe that anyone, of *any* race, could just get up and walk away without a tremendous amount of emotional and mental work. How can anyone who believes that Black and Mexican children *belong* in ghettos help them get out?

I learned that college alone is not what teaches people to see. It is only those with the willingness to look beneath the surface and honestly examine the brutal reality that shapes a ghetto child who will learn to see.

25

Destroy the Mother, Destroy the Child

A small transistor radio always hung from a shoulder strap on my mother's side and tiny earphones were permanent fixtures in her ears. Radio talk shows and classical music were her constant companions. A collection of old classical record albums and sheet music accompanied my mother into Aliso Village. She acquired them and professional voice lessons during her marriage to my father. My mother had an exceptional voice.

One afternoon, Sandra's mother entered our back door and was startled by the deep, vibrating operatic voice of Mario Lanza roaring through our tiny apartment. She shouted, "What kinda of music you *playing*, girl? That music like to put me to *sleep!*"

My mother's musical preferences were not the only thing that strikingly contrasted her from Aliso Village. Her intense interest in books probably would have made her stand out even in the world outside the ghetto. Books abundantly filled every available corner in our tiny apartment. Even the kitchen cabinets were crowded with books in and around cans and containers of food. Books were an extremely important part of my mother's life.

I need to emphasize that my mother had more than just a healthy desire to learn. She had an insatiable hunger for knowledge that compulsively drove her from one book to another. There was a frantic urgency to find the things through books she so desperately needed in her life.

She did gain an enormous awareness of herself and other people. As a child, I came to realize and respect the power books have to change people's perceptions and attitudes. However, my mother was unable to use her vast knowledge because she lacked the direction and, more importantly, the self-respect to do so. Her experiences during the time she lived in Aliso drained her self-esteem to a level of emptiness that I do not think she even recognized or understood.

The alcoholism that resulted from the constant abuse by people in authority began to ravish my mother, slowly taking her away — piece by piece — and leaving behind only a skeleton of what she once was. Part of me died with her . . . that spiritual umbilical cord that connects us to our mothers became frayed and unraveled, leaving me sailing on turbulent waters without a compass.

My mother did seek professional help. I remember how relieved I was that someone was finally going to help with her problems. The afternoon after her first visit, she returned home and burst through the front door in tears. I followed her into the bedroom. My mother was told the only reason that she was even being considered for professional help was for the sake of her children. They made it painfully clear that they had no interest in her as a person.

At this time in my mother's life, one word of encouragement by any of these so-called professionals whom she highly respected would have meant so much. Instead, she was treated with rejection and contempt by the same people who supposedly became professionals in the social welfare fields to assist people with their problems. I will never forget the hypocrisy that did so much damage to my mother.

I once read a beautiful pearl of wisdom: "Rudeness is a weak person's imitation of strength." Perhaps, if my mother had understood the concept behind those words, she would have been able to evaluate others more accurately and see them for what they really were. Instead, my mother measured her self-worth by the constant diet of rejection and contempt from those who called themselves "professionals."

✳ ✳

My mother's condition rapidly deteriorated and began to manifest itself in the form of disappearances: first, they were one-day weekend disappearances; gradually, they became two and three days.

Sometimes the welfare check would come in the mail during one of my mother's disappearances. My brother Mike would take a nail file and carefully remove the thin, white envelope from the mailbox. (It was very important to immediately remove the check because it would otherwise be stolen within hours after its delivery.)

I was thirteen when my mother's disappearances began. It was the most frightening during the night, knowing that no adult was in the house to protect us from unforeseen circumstances or dangers. When my mother did return, she would always explain that she was across town "taking care of business." No one dared to question her further for fear that she would completely abandon us as our father had done.

Food was often sparse during these disappearances — I recall sharing a jar of peanut butter for dinner with my sisters and brothers. Sometimes my mother would experience one of her fits of rage upon returning home. We would all take refuge in our bedroom and wait until the storm subsided. I learned to control the frantic terror I felt inside.

In the recesses of my mind, I saw a wounded child filled with terror huddled in a tiny corner. Fragile, like a bird with broken wings, she was trapped — not so much by the metal bars of her cage, but by the *mental* bars that had escaped her sight and touch, and deeply lodged themselves in her mind. Each time she attempted to reach through them, the invisible bars gripped her tighter and held her back.

26

Cold Turkey

Angela and I slowly mounted the creaky stairs to the wooden house that belonged to her in-laws. As we entered through an old screen door, the sounds of agonizing pain echoed from the long hallway towards the kitchen.

We both moved closer and I saw three Mexican teenage boys standing over the body of a young girl. They worked feverishly to hold her down as her drug-induced convulsive body violently tossed. The three young men were wearing darkly colored jeans and no shirts. All I could see were their bare backs and flexing muscles as they struggled to keep the young girl pinned on top of the bed. The whole room seemed to shake as the unnatural contortions developed on her face. She clawed at the bare backs of the men holding her down, trying to protect her from herself.

Excruciating pain tormented her as she continued to screech out in agony. In spite of her petite stature (less than one hundred and five pounds), the physical force of her pain almost over-whelmed that of three well-built teenage boys. Moments following each withdrawal, her twisted expressions would relax and the face of a young girl drained of all energy would appear ... a child desperately fighting for her life.

It frightened me to the deepest core of my soul to watch the ominous power of drugs take complete control of this girl's body; I was sure she was going to die.

* *

In ghettos, most people will not seek rehabilitation centers when they need help. They learn from early experiences of watching their loved ones suffer or die that no one cares what happens to them. Many of these young people try to handle enormous medical problems alone and often unnecessarily lose their lives. This is a reality brought about by the way ghetto children learn to see the world: they learn to feel they are not included. Those feelings are clearly reflected in the way they choose to handle their lives.

27

When Feelings Die

I boarded the crowded bus early one afternoon and headed for downtown Los Angeles. I gently pushed through the mass of people standing in the aisle and made my way to a tiny space near the rear door. As more people continued boarding, I quickly became crammed up against the door. The bus pulled out to leave and I noticed a sign: "Do not stand near rear door. It is dangerous." No one else seemed to notice the sign or the four-teen-year-old girl crammed up against the door. Even the bus driver, who had a full view of me, did nothing to ensure my safety.

Images of my life quickly raced through my mind: bullets flying over my head at ten; Dorothy profusely bleeding to death on my front yard at thirteen; pimps' shiny new cars lining the parking lots every weekend; prostitutes dancing on our ceiling until the early morning hours; users cooking their drugs on a spoon under the stairwells. A steaming volcano of emotion threatened to rup-ture within me as I examined the blank expressions of most of the adults seated on the bus.

112

All the things that deeply disturbed me about my life seemed to be oblivious to them. They did not care if I fell out of the door of that bus, I felt . . . *they were dead,* I thought . . . their feelings were gone, I believed. This realization sent a cold chill through my spine.

＊＊

I dismounted the bus and disappeared into the ever-present crowds lining the streets of downtown Los Angeles. I felt a thin layer of thick soot begin to cake on my face. I aimlessly wandered into a small corner store where bright sunlight reflected on watches in a glass case near a window. Their sparkle flashed in the corner of my eye; a sudden darkness loomed within . . . a strange sensation of loss.

A profound numbness rippled through me as I instantly realized that I could no longer cry. Panic-stricken, I could not grasp what was happening. With a deep feeling of urgency, I understood that I had to cry there and then, or never cry again for rest of my life.

Instinctively, and to no avail, I reached inside to bring up the tears. There I was: flanked by a throng of people in the middle of a busy store in downtown Los Angeles, trying to make myself cry. Physically, I was standing; emotionally, I was on my knees begging God to return what I had lost. There, in front of all those people, the tears finally began to pour down my face. I was too deeply relieved to feel embarrassed.

28

Through the Eyes of the Media

It was a lively party. Teenagers, most of whom Angela and I knew, crowded the tiny Aliso apartment. Music loudly blared from two large speakers placed at opposite ends of the living room. Some of the young men and women were dancing in the center of the living room; some were seated on two long sofas.

I was sitting at a tiny, metal kitchen table talking to my friend, Bear — a husky Hispanic teenager whom I had known for a long time. We were talking about his after-school job as an orderly for a small, private hospital located across the street from Aliso Village. He was trying to help his mother, who was struggling to raise him and his brother alone, and gave her almost all of his paycheck. It was very touching to watch his gentle eyes convey the deep affection he held for his mother.

In the midst of our conversation, a handful of tiny pills was suddenly thrown on the table in front of me. I looked up in total surprise as a young man I had never seen before ordered me to take one. His eyes were beet red as he stumbled through his words a second time, ordering me to take a pill. "Cut the virgin act and *take the damn pill!*"

Bear suddenly stood up — towering far above him — and roared, "Fuck off, man. Kathy don't do that shit!" I was trembling because I was sure a knife or a gun was coming out next. Instead, the intoxicated teenager just hobbled off into one of the bedrooms in the apartment.

✳ ✳

One evening following the incident at the party, a news bulletin flashed across our television screen: a vivid description of a sick and vicious killer. It was loudly announced that a police officer had been killed in Aliso Village by a deadly, armed and dangerous person. I gasped in total disbelief when a picture of Bear appeared.

If people are innocent until proven guilty, than why was a public annihilation of Bear's character broadcast before he was given the opportunity to prove his innocence? I named this chapter "Through the Eyes of the Media" because the media were the only eyes through which the public was allowed to see Bear.

Let this story be the eyes that saw the person Bear was before the tragedy of growing up in the ghetto came to claim him and his only brother, who was killed in the ghetto at fourteen.

PART VII

Institutionalized Illiteracy: The Academic Dumping Grounds

29

Underprivileged

The warm sunshine caressed my arms and a gentle breeze tickled the back of my neck as I scurried off to school. I carefully stepped around the bright yellow wild flowers that peeked out from under the cracks in the sidewalk. I went directly to my homeroom and was told to report to the attendance office.

When I arrived, I was instructed to wait in another office where a large desk was cluttered with pens, pencils, note pads, a calendar and several stacks of manila folders. Piled highly on one of the stacks was a folder with "Underprivileged" penciled in next to my name. I carefully examined the unfamiliar word which conjured up all sorts of vivid images: Aliso Village; the drab green brick walls that towered into the air; the multitude of women and children whose apartments were sandwiched between the three stories of each building; the tiny spaces they called home.

A man walked into the office, opened my folder and casually darted a long list of very personal questions at me. One question that embarrassed me the most required telling him that my father did not visit or sleep in my mother's bed or mine. I felt like my clothes had been ripped off before a jeering crowd of people.

✳ ✳

When I arrived home from school that afternoon, I went straight for the dictionary and quickly thumbed through the words that began with the letter "U."

There it was: "deprived, as through social or economic oppression, of some of the fundamental rights of all members of a civilized society."

Fundamental rights. Suddenly the justification for the harsh reality of the ghetto became crystal clear . . . the ambulances that refused to come and the ones that showed up two and one-half hours later . . . the doctors that sent sick babies home to die . . . the schools that misidentified Angela and others like her as "slow learners" to provide justification for herding them into classrooms without teachers . . . the sexually molested children and the police who looked the other way.

Now it all made sense to me. I could see the logic in it. Those who treated ghetto people without respect or dignity did so because they clearly understood the definition of the word "underprivileged" and based their behavior on its clear-cut definition.

30

Respect for Property

Our first art project was to construct an Easter bunny from egg cartons, construction paper, cotton, paint, glue and tissue paper. After much patience and care, I put together an intricate piece of work for which my art teacher, Mrs. Brown, highly praised me. I was informed the following day that my efforts had earned me the highest grade in the class: A+!

I beamed with pride and thanked my teacher for her esteemed evaluation of my work. However, Mrs. Brown wanted to know if she could sell my Easter project at an art fair she was attending that weekend. I explained to her that my project was made as a gift for my mother. Mrs. Brown pressed on and asked me if she could take it just for the purpose of display. She pushed harder as she told me that she wanted her friends to see it because she was so proud of my work. I finally gave my permission.

All that weekend I worried about my art project. What if it was damaged at the fair? I wanted so much to present it to my mother as an Easter gift to communicate how much I loved her. The following Monday, as I hurried through the door of my art class hoping to find my art project, I was met with disappointment. My eyes darted across the room in search of it; all I could see was an empty counter.

Moments later, Mrs. Brown entered the classroom. I looked at her for an explanation but none was forthcoming. She simply walked over and handed me two quarters.

I was perplexed. "What is this for?"

She curtly responded, "Your art project."

The two, icy cold pieces of metal in my hand sharply contrasted the blood coming to a boil in my veins. As my anger reached a fever pitch, I thrust the two quarters directly at Mrs. Brown, hitting her in the back, and screamed, *"You lying bitch!"*

Two men escorted me to the principal's office and my mother was called. Through the paper-thin walls, I heard the principal tell her that I lacked self-control. He informed my mother that Mrs. Brown was an outstanding teacher with an impeccable record, and her honesty and integrity were beyond reproach.

∗ ∗

How do ghetto children learn to have respect for other people's property when authority figures demonstrate a complete lack of respect for *their* property? Children do learn what they live.

31

Out of Tune

My love for music was initiated by my mother's beautiful singing voice. I remember, when I was three, looking up at her as she sang the original version of "Summertime." She held her notes so beautifully; her voice almost had the depth of an opera singer. When my father came home from work, I sometimes sang "Sugar In The Morning," a famous song of the fifties.

I was very excited about taking a music class at Hollenbeck. As I entered the class, I noticed all the seats situated in rows descending in height towards the front of the classroom. A very large, middle-aged Caucasian man slowly sauntered in. Moments after he formally introduced himself as being our instructor, he began discussing some of his personal and financial motivations for choosing to come to a school like ours. Music was never mentioned.

Day after day, our instructor discussed his tax returns, the price of his home, his wife and children's personal problems, and his custom of doing all of the grocery shopping for them. It was during one of these drawn-out, inappropriate discussions that

Manuel, one of the boys in our class, blurted out, "Do you buy your wife's Kotex, too?"

All the other boys roared with laughter; the girls remained dead silent. In anger, our instructor ordered the young man to come down to the front of the class and take a tiny piece of paper to the principal's office.

In defiance, Manuel ripped it up and challenged the instructor to meet him outside. "Maybe you could start earning some of that extra money you get paid for working at *a school like ours,* man!" Manuel roared from outside the classroom. "Man, you sure the hell don't earn it in *this* class. I've been sitting in your class for eight fucking weeks and you ain't taught anybody *shit* about music. I didn't come to this fucking class to learn about your family. You're full of *shit,* man! You want to suspend me? Go *ahead,* man!"

Manuel was back in school the very next day seated right behind me, his foot impatiently thumping against the leg of his chair. Our instructor opened the class with a discussion about college-bound programs. "I do not believe in free lunches!" he proudly announced. "If you cannot afford to go to college, you simply do not go. No one gave *me* a free college education. My parents paid for my education out of their own pockets."

With a strange smile on his face, he looked around at all the girls in the class. "Most of you will be mothers before you're even out of high school." All the girls dropped their heads in embarrassment. "Anyway, it takes a certain kind of person to make it in college . . . it takes a strength of character that growing up in this area could never nurture in most people."

With those words, Manuel kicked the leg of his chair and a loud thud permeated the room. He then picked up a chair sitting in the corner of the room (since ours were nailed to the floor) and, with tremendous force, flung it at the instructor. Just in time and in complete horror, the instructor jumped out of the way of the chair.

Enraged, Manuel rushed towards the instructor and yanked him by the arm outside the classroom. We all heard the instructor plead with Manuel to talk this thing out.

"Talk this thing out? You don't think I got the balls to make it through college, man! Is that what you're trying to tell me in your fucking class? *Fuck you,* man!" The next thing we heard was an enormous thud as our instructor fell to the ground after being punched in the face.

Several inquiring school administrators rushed into our classroom . . . no one said a word.

32

The Exception to the Rule

I hastened into the classroom while the school bell was ringing. I picked a seat in the last row in the back of the class and checked my class schedule against what was written on the blackboard: eighth grade math. I was in the right classroom. A middle-aged Oriental man with a firm but friendly demeanor entered. He printed "Mr. Honda" on the blackboard and our math lesson began.

Mr. Honda introduced the concept of mathematical equations. He explained how important it was to start at the beginning of a math concept and learn it one step at a time. He always invited us to ask questions, constantly stressed how important questions were when we failed to understand something, and often mentioned that questions were the seeds to learning and mastering any concept.

I was accustomed to teachers who implied that you should be able to open the book and learn it yourself ... an attitude I had come to expect at Hollenbeck. Mr. Honda abruptly broke that mold. He printed numbers across the blackboard and clearly showed me how to use them in a variety of ways. I began to immensely enjoy working with numbers and sat more towards the front of the class. As my confidence began to grow, I felt eager to learn with each new lesson.

One afternoon, Mr. Honda asked me to do a math problem on the board in front of the class. All the steps were very clear to me. I glanced over at Mr. Honda for approval.

"Outstanding work!" he shouted. I felt as though my mind had been given wings and could freely soar through any mathematical equation in the world because Mr. Honda believed in me. I felt so proud of the "A" I received in math that semester because I knew, behind that grade, I had honestly learned something.

I rushed home that afternoon, hurried through the front door and saw my mother preparing dinner. Beaming with pride, I handed her my beautiful report card. She took it in her hand and turned her back to me as she silently read it. I anxiously waited for her response but none was forthcoming.

When she finally turned around, she handed back my report card, completely ignoring my "A" in math, and reminded me to wash my hands before dinner. I felt deeply confused and upset as I carefully put away my special report card in a safe place.

I returned to school the next morning deeply depressed but, as I entered Mr. Honda's class, my depression began to dissipate. He asked me to stay after class and sit in the chair next to his desk. He told me that I was one of his best students and informed me that he was aware I lived in Aliso Village. He tried to impress upon me that I could get out of Aliso Village. He said I had a very good mind and could do anything I wanted in life.

* *

During elementary school, I had good teachers. However, when I reached junior high school, all that changed. Mr. Honda was the only teacher I found at Hollenbeck who really attempted to teach me anything.

As I continued my academic journey to Roosevelt, the situation grew worse. Mr. Honda's class had given me the rare opportunity to demonstrate to myself that I was not lazy *or* stupid, and had the strength to reject these negative messages constantly being conveyed to me.

Mr. Honda made a difference in my life because good teachers plant the seeds for change.

33

Mixed Messages

It was a chilly night. My mother and I walked to Hollenbeck Junior High School for my counseling appointment to address the issue of my plummeting grades. I just did not care anymore; almost all of my classes were a joke.

When we arrived at Hollenbeck, we were taken into an office and greeted by a friendly school counselor. My mother politely asked, "Are there any available tutorial programs to help Kathleen improve her grades?"

"Well, Mrs. Bishop," the school counselor said, sitting back in his padded office chair and making himself more comfortable, "I don't think this young lady needs a tutorial program." With that strange smile — just like my music teacher wore when he suggested to the girls in our class that they would probably become mothers before they even finished high school — he flirtatiously eyed my body and remarked, "A girl that looks like *that* doesn't need to worry about her grades."

My mother was stunned. She abruptly grabbed my arm, briskly escorted me out of his office, and headed down the corridor to the building exit. I felt her anger quietly burning as I quickly trailed behind her fast-paced walk. I wondered how she would respond if she knew about what *really* went on in most of my classes . . . I was afraid to tell her the truth.

I was angry at my mother for ignoring my academic achievements during the semester I had Mr. Honda — the only teacher at Hollenbeck that had ever taught me anything. I was angry at the school counselor for demonstrating a complete lack of respect for me in front of my mother. I kept reaching for the logic; because there was none, I became more frustrated and confused.

34

Roosevelt Walkouts

I slowly sauntered into my new algebra class and gaped at the algebra instructor: his feet were propped up on his desk while he read a paperback novel. Some students talked aimlessly; others cracked jokes and freely passed out drugs in the form of tiny red pills referred to as "reds." I pulled out a piece of notebook paper, brought for the purpose of algebra, and began sketching the pathetic world around me.

I studied the instructor's vacant eyes as they remained glued to the novel and oblivious to the chaotic condition of his class. I carefully examined his slouched posture and placement of his legs and feet, carelessly and freely pointed towards the ceiling from atop his desk. As this absurd image of an educator took form in my sketches, it was as if I were drawing a comic strip, only the characters were real and the reality far from a joke.

The frightening truth was that every person in that class, for whatever reason, had been abandoned and dropped into the academic dumping grounds of Roosevelt High School.

I had been left to intellectually die and was perceptive enough to recognize it. That was when I began considering the possibility of dropping out of high school.

✳ ✳

I vividly remember the day I pressed through the crowds of angry students walking out of their classes in protest. Trash cans were set ablaze all over the school. The overwhelming whirlpool of frustration I shared with all of these students had reached a fever pitch as students began chanting slogans and demanding change.

The walkouts grew so enormous that they caught the attention of the media. The newspapers ran numerous articles about the walkouts and the many inner-city schools finally taking a stand against the deteriorating conditions of their educational systems. At the top of the list were the attitudes and actions of teachers and school administrators.

> *Los Angeles Times*, March 15, 1969, Page 1, Part II: "At Roosevelt High School in East Los Angeles, about 45 Mexican-American students crowded into the principal's office to demand a Chicano principal for the school. The group called for a Mexican-American curriculum and removal of racist teachers. 'We will sit here as long as we have to,' said Grace Reis, 18, coordinator of the campus Brown Beret movement. 'We will resort to violence if necessary: violence is all they understand.'"

Today I see that the inner-city schools not only continue to have a deteriorating educational system but now, instead of walking out of classes or dropping out of school, students are packing guns and going to school to kill.

Ghetto children kill because they have been destroyed by an educational system that continues to keep them illiterate, social workers that often fail to report child abuse, police that commonly fail to protect children from abuse, a legal system that has repeatedly looked the other way, and a society that has long denied the reality that a ghetto child even exists.

A mind is not only a terrible thing to waste, it is a *dangerous* thing to waste. It is only when ghetto children are honestly offered the opportunity to develop their minds that they will learn to embrace life instead of death.

Part VIII

Beyond Childhood: They Take The Ghetto With Them

35

Job Corps

The idea came to me one afternoon as I was watching a television advertisement for Job Corps. I envisioned Job Corps as the solution to my problems — it would at least provide me with vocational training so that I would be prepared to work when I graduated. I felt Roosevelt had not provided me with an academic education or vocational training. It seemed clear to me that I had nothing to lose by dropping out of high school and joining Job Corps.

The following evening I announced to my mother, "I am going to drop out of high school to join Job Corps."

"Drop out of high school? Are you *crazy?*"

"Why do you think everyone is walking out of their classes at Roosevelt?" I asked. "Angela doesn't even have any *teachers* in her classes! I don't know what Roosevelt is, but it is not a school for me or most of the people I know! I am dropping out and *that's final!*" I ran to my bedroom and slammed the door shut. My mother very reluctantly agreed to let me go.

✶ ✶

As I boarded the old Greyhound bus leaving Los Angeles for Oregon I felt, for the first time in my life, the strange sensation of being alone. I curiously watched the Los Angeles roads and buildings disappear into the distance as we pulled out of the station.

I emerged from the bus to find a military base surrounded by the Columbia River. Uniformed guards were stationed at the entrance as we waited for clearance to the base. A massive, two-story brick building served as our living quarters. I shared a room and a large bathroom lined with private toilets and showers with three other girls on the first floor of the building. We were each assigned our own metal cot and metal locker. Meals were served three times a day in the cafeteria. We attended vocational training classes. I also chose to work on my General Education Requirements (G.E.D.).

I began receiving letters from a boy at Roosevelt — the brother of a girl with whom I had shared lockers. His letters were friendly and comforting.

An episode that deeply bothered me took place shortly after I arrived. All three of the girls with whom I shared a room had gone out on a weekend pass. (I chose not to go with them because I knew, growing up in Aliso, that I would probably find drugs waiting for me and no friends to protect me from being forced to take them.) As I lay on my bed listening to one of the girls share her weekend experiences, a deep sense of fear and sorrow engulfed me. Her dull, hazel-brown eyes showed no hint of emotion as she described in graphic detail how three teenage boys performed oral, vaginal, and rectal sex on her. The nonchalant way she spoke about herself, as though she were just a piece of trash being tossed about between guys, deeply saddened me.

One evening I decided to stroll along an old wooden dock on base near some water, perhaps searching for some small space where I could escape the craziness all around me. It was a serene place, completely undisturbed by noise or the usual chaos that seemed to follow me everywhere. As I slowly sauntered along this deserted dock, I gradually began to experience the most unfamiliar feeling: for the first time since my father had abandoned me, I felt safe. It was a beautiful, glorious feeling that only flickered for a brief moment, but how I relished that precious moment of peace!

I met a girl named Rosario. She was born and raised in Bolivia and spoke English well. We became very good friends and, for the first time in Job Corps, I began to have fun. Rosario and I ran laps after classes in an old airplane hanger and timed each other; sometimes we hiked in nearby hills and picked blackberries.

Rosario and I befriended an older woman named Mrs. Brown, a nursing aide instructor at Job Corps. Mrs. Brown allowed Rosario and me to bake pies at her home from the blackberries we collected in the hills. Mrs. Brown had many books about nutrition and loaned some to me. I learned a great deal about carbohydrates and proteins, and how to combine foods in your diet to control weight.

During one of these visits, I was eagerly glancing through one of Mrs. Brown's books and felt her staring at me. It made me uncomfortable as I slowly glanced up to meet her gaze. With sincere concern in her voice, she gingerly asked, "How could your mother let you come to Job Corps all by yourself?"

When I remained silent, I felt her growing impatience. She blurted out a second question that I, as a sixteen-year-old, lacked the mental development to fully understand and the emotional maturity to answer.

"Is your mother *crazy?*" Still a child, my first response was a protective one towards my mother. I stubbornly remained silent.

I do not think Mrs. Brown asked the question with malice. She honestly could not understand how my mother could let a sixteen-year-old girl travel all the way to Job Corps alone. It was unimaginable to Mrs. Brown that the circumstances of my life would force me to seek Job Corps as a refuge. We lived in different worlds. I ended my friendship with Mrs. Brown because I felt that she would never believe the reality of my life, much less understand it.

* *

My studies were coming along well. I was proudly typing seventy words per minute and mastering all the office skills I needed to develop in order to complete my vocational training program. I was almost prepared to take my G.E.D. test.

One afternoon we were presented with a battery of tests, the objective of which were not explained. The week following the test, I was notified to report to the administration office. I timidly entered the office and a man seated behind a desk asked me to take a seat. He inquired why I joined Job Corps.

Defensively I responded, "Because of the walkouts at my high school."

" Walkouts?"

As I briefly explained the situation at Roosevelt, his eyes widened with surprise and he held up a folder. "Did you know that you have reading comprehension scores far above the national average in this country?"

I was truly shocked and stood there looking at him in total amazement. *How can that be?* I thought. I had been told by my counselors that I was only a little above average in intelligence and would probably not make it in college. *This must be a mistake,* I thought. I looked up at the man. "Are you sure?"

"I am absolutely sure! I think you should *definitely* go to college. You have a lot of potential that should be developed."

I could not believe my ears. I dropped out of high school to end up hearing this? Concrete reading comprehension scores had never been made known to me at Roosevelt or Hollenbeck. Why? Where was the logic in all of this?

Out of my anger, I developed an iron-will determination to go to college and graduate. I decided that I would never rely on someone else's assessment of my abilities. I would test my own abilities against reality instead of blindly accepting someone else's opinion as fact. It was one of the most important lessons I would ever learn.

36

Racism Outside the Ghetto

As I looked up at the massive brick buildings of Aliso Village, they appeared smaller and less intimidating than before. The tiny stores that dotted First Street seemed more like the artificial props in a play than the authentic backdrop of anyone's life. Everything had changed; I no longer saw the ghetto through the eyes of a child.

During my one-week visit home, I dated a Hispanic boy (we will call him Ramon) whom I had met at Roosevelt and from whom I received several letters while in Job Corps. On the day I was to return, he escorted me to the Greyhound bus station. We were very intrigued with the tiny, coin-operated mini-televisions attached to the arms of the seats in the station.

I went to check my bus ticket. Upon my return, I found Ramon being entertained by one of the mini-televisions. His eyes were glued to the tiny screen vividly displaying an entire football field. I playfully moved my hand in front of the screen, attempting to break his concentration, and accidently slipped and fell in his lap. As we both laughed, an angry voice encroached upon us.

I reluctantly looked up and saw a Black security guard clutching the handle of the gun that hung on his side. "Do you have butt problems?" he asked me.

I think Ramon instinctively felt that if he said one word in my defense, this man would instantly shoot both of us dead. The Black guard smiled at his success in humiliating Ramon in front of a woman . . . a White woman.

**

It was an unfortunate experience that Ramon and I tried to put behind us. Little did we realize that it was just a glimpse into our future if we wanted to conduct an interracial relationship. Nothing could have prepared us for the road that stood ahead and the irrevocable damage it would do to our lives.

37

Born in East L.A.

It was an early summer evening. The hazy sun glared through the window panes . . . my eighteenth birthday. I now lived in my own Pasadena apartment with a female roommate and had graduated from Job Corps. During six months of night school, I earned an official high school diploma from Pasadena High School and was registered for Pasadena City College beginning in September. I worked full time as a clerk typist for a small company in a temporary job designed to give me job experience. My life was finally in order; I felt like I knew where I was going. Most importantly, my eighteenth birthday marked the beginning of my adulthood.

My roommate was out of town that weekend visiting her mother. I remember being home alone in the early evening. I was preparing something to eat when I heard an unexpected knock at the door. Ramon presented me with a birthday gift and I invited him in. We laughed and talked for a few hours. Then it grew unusually silent and our kissing suddenly became extremely passionate. Things got out of control . . . it just happened.

I had dreamt that my first time would be the most beautiful experience in my life — not this unceremoniously hurried event. I ran into the bedroom closet and closed the door. Cloaked in the darkness, I slowly lowered myself to the floor and tears ran down my face.

Ramon finally knocked. I said nothing as I dressed myself in the gray shadows. In a state of deep emotional conflict and confusion, I emerged. I was truly dazed as we both walked to the bus stop.

In Ramon's perception, there was nothing wrong with what we had done; in my perception, we had done something that I felt was deeply wrong. I thought about Robert and Armando. They always made me feel special for being a virgin, while Ramon made me feel silly and childish. I suddenly missed Robert and Armando; Ramon and I both agreed to end our relationship.

✶ ✶

I began attending Pasadena City College the following month. I wanted to put my experience with Ramon behind me and go on with my life. Two months later, terror struck: I missed my period for a second time. There seemed to be a Planned Parenthood Clinic on every Pasadena corner in the early seventies. I nervously approached the entrance to one of them and peeked through the front door, forcing myself to continue walking into the facility. As I reached the receptionist desk, I awkwardly asked in a low whisper, "I would like to take a pregnancy test."

The receptionist loudly responded, "You want to take a *pregnancy test*?" Deeply embarrassed, I quickly shook my head.

In a small room, blood was extracted from my arm; I was told to wait for the results. A young woman emerged from one of the offices, walked towards me and informed me that I was pregnant. Tears streamed down my face as I felt for the first time the full gravity of my dilemma.

The woman that worked at the clinic looked down at me. "Don't cry. Just come into my office and we can discuss some solutions." I followed her down the hall and into her office. She pulled out some papers and began suggesting abortion as the solution to my problem. I felt that I had engaged in an act, however regrettably, that produced a human life. There was a tiny, defenseless person flourishing inside of me. I suddenly felt a tremendous responsibility for this life that had been placed in my hands.

With those thoughts and feelings, my decision was made. I arose from the chair. The woman behind the desk asked, "When would you like to make an appointment for your abortion?"

"I have decided not to have an abortion." She seemed genuinely puzzled. Without another word, I walked out the door.

I entered the nearest phone booth, nervously slipped the coins into the slots and apprehensively dialed Ramon's phone number. It was over between us and I wanted it to remain that way. However, I felt it was dishonorable to have an illegitimate child. I repeatedly rehearsed what I would say when I announced to him that I was pregnant with his child, but all my rehearsals did not prepare me for the real thing.

When Ramon finally answered the phone, my voice barely squeaked out an introduction. I could tell he was surprised to hear from me. With a tremendous effort, I finally worked up enough courage to tell him that I was pregnant.

"We only did it one time!" he yelled. The phone instantly dropped from my hand; I dazed at the mouthpiece freely dangling in the air. I could hear Ramon shouting through the phone, "Are you OK?"

I wandered aimlessly out of the phone booth, certain that Ramon was going to abandon me like so many other people had in my life. To my surprise, Ramon showed up at my apartment about an hour and a half later to propose marriage.

✳ ✳

The Los Angeles County Court House was very crowded on the day of our marriage. We were the only teenagers among the many middle-aged people waiting in line for a marriage license. When our names were finally called, we were married in a hurried, no-frills ceremony that lasted less than five minutes. I moved in with Ramon's parents while Ramon continued attending Cal Lutheran College in Thousand Oaks. Ramon had been an honor student in high school and had earned a fully paid scholarship.

I took a job as a salesgirl at Soto Drug Store in East Los Angeles to earn enough money for my prenatal care and maternity expenses. I chose a small, private hospital within walking distance from Ramon's parent's house. I could only afford the plan that required me to see whatever doctor was on call. Unlike the county hospital, this facility was immaculate; no beds lined any of the hallways. The doctors seemed indifferent as they hurried down the halls, but I reasoned that they were just busy doing their jobs.

I felt completely confident with my decision to have my baby there. I carried a great deal of shame about growing up on welfare and did not want to start my life with my hand held out. I felt so proud of the fact that I had earned the money to pay for my prenatal care and delivery. I did not ask for a free lunch.

As I waited for the birth of my child, my husband was having great difficulty coping with the predominantly White environment at Cal Lutheran College. There was an incident where a serious fight erupted and my husband lost a few teeth. When I tried to encourage him to share his experience with me, he snapped. "Why do you want to know everything that is going on inside of me?" As he shut the door on me, a wall grew between us.

＊ ＊

On May 14, 1972, I woke up to mild contractions slowly vibrating across my lower abdomen. I showered and dressed in preparation to go to the hospital, knowing instinctively that my baby would be born that day. It was Sunday — Mother's Day. As we entered the hospital, I signed in and was handed a hospital gown; my husband was sent to a waiting area.

I was placed on an examination table with my legs in metal stirrups. A Black doctor peeked into the entrance of the room. As he approached, he examined my left hand for a wedding ring and acidly asked, "Aren't you even *married?*" (My fingers were too swollen for me to wear my wedding ring due to the pregnancy.) I was stunned by his question and remained silent out of anger.

The doctor then ordered a nurse to help me off the table and take me to the showers. I was experiencing pains in my lower abdomen as I removed my hospital gown and stepped into the shower. I was left there unattended. As I struggled to remain standing under the running water, a sharp jolt of pain in my lower abdomen knocked me to the floor and I lost consciousness. When I awoke, I was in a darkened room on a twin-size hospital bed, unable to remember how or when I got there.

Moments later, a nurse entered the room and inserted a long, plastic syringe into my body to rupture the water sack. Water began gushing out everywhere as my contractions rapidly intensified. Sharp, thrusting pains overwhelmed me as I screamed out for help. My husband appeared over my bed and looked down at me. "You are not trying hard enough." When he turned and walked out of the room, I realized he was more afraid than I was.

A Black woman came into the room at some point and began mopping up the water from beneath my bed. A White doctor appeared in the doorway complaining that I was making too much noise.

The Black woman walked over to my bed, took hold of my right hand and said, "You scream all you want, child, 'cause I ain't seen *one* of them men doctors gonna get up on *this* bed and have *him* a baby and don't make no *noise!*"

A faint smile formed on my lips as my lower abdomen continued to twist in excruciating pain, finally causing me to succumb to unconsciousness. Sometime later, I awoke to bright surgical lights painfully banging against my eyes. I was immediately turned on my left side and a large needle was slowly inserted into my spine. A short while later, all sensation from my waist down completely disappeared.

A White doctor whom I had never seen was to deliver my baby; the Black doctor who had examined me earlier was to assist him. The Black doctor placed his hands on my abdomen, felt my contractions and instructed me when to push; the White doctor stood at the end of the table holding a long, metal pair of pincers, observing my cervix.

As I pushed, I did not know that I was severely tearing my vaginal walls — neither did both of these doctors. When my baby finally crowned, the White doctor tightly squeezed the metal forceps against her temples and began to forcibly yank her out of my body.

During my pregnancy, I had so often imagined what it would be like when my baby was born. Like most mothers, I imagined the doctor spanking her tiny bottom as she announced her arrival into the world with a loud and boisterously healthy cry. When my baby finally made her entrance into the world, an unnatural silence fell upon the room. Immediately alarmed (like any mother would be), I frantically waited for a cry, a sound ... anything but the dead silence that paralyzed me with overwhelming dread. Her motionless body held no hint of life as she dangled from the palm of the White doctor's hand. When the White doctor finally announced that she was just asleep, I experienced an overwhelming relief.

He handed my newborn to the nurse who immediately wrapped her in a blanket and hurriedly removed her from the delivery room. I wanted so much to hold her, to touch her, to smell her — but this precious moment was ripped away from me.

Suddenly I heard the Black doctor yell, "The mother is bleeding profusely and I cannot stop it!"

The White doctor yelled back, "We better stop the bleeding or she will go into shock!" Immediately, several nurses came rushing into the delivery room. I could hear the echo of my blood striking the edges of the stainless steel bowl that was placed on the floor near the delivery table.

The two doctors worked frantically to pack my vaginal canal with enough ice to slow down the hemorrhaging. I tasted my warm, salty tears as they trickled down my face. The desire to sleep overwhelmed me, but a nurse cautioned me to stay awake.

A large clock faced me in the delivery room. I used it as a focal point to try and keep myself alert. I counted the seconds and minutes until they became hours. Two and one-half hours following my daughter's birth, I was still in the delivery room undergoing surgery. The two doctors were gingerly sewing the lacerations as the ice slowed down the bleeding.

I was finally rolled out of the delivery room and my in-laws were waiting outside in anxious anticipation. When I was placed into the recovery room my husband approached me, his dread permeating the room. "Why were you in there so long? I thought you had died and they didn't want to tell me."

I faintly responded, *"Never again!"*

The following morning, my daughter was rolled into my room at about five o'clock. As I looked into the tiny glass bed, she opened her soft, green eyes and looked at me. Her delicate mouth curled up at both ends; her dainty hands and feet waved aimlessly in the air. As I held her for the first time, it was so difficult for me to believe that something so precious and beautiful could really belong to me.

As I prepared to leave the hospital, I developed a pounding headache. The Black doctor who had assisted in delivering my baby entered my hospital room. Instead of being sarcastic, he rubbed his hands together in a nervous fashion and warned me, "If you start bleeding, don't wait around." He turned and walked out of the room without any further explanation.

✳ ✳

Several days after I returned home, I was still not feeling well. I continued to experience nausea but no bleeding. My mother-in-law prepared oatmeal (Mexican style) cooked with cinnamon sticks and milk — the only thing that I could keep in my stomach.

My mother came to help me with my new baby. When she saw that I was not feeling well, she suggested that I stay with her for a few days. (It was nine days since my daughter's birth.) My mother shook me out of my sleep early the following morning with horror outlined on her face. I immediately felt the warm blood soaking my clothes beneath me. Frantically, I lifted myself up only to discover more blood quickly gushing out.

My mother packed me with sanitary napkins to slow down the blood flow. She chose to call my in-laws to take me to the hospital rather than an ambulance because of the two and one-half hours it usually took ambulances to arrive at Aliso Village. My brother-in-law quickly arrived and raced me to the emergency entrance of the hospital where my daughter had been born. Immediately upon arrival, I was rushed into emergency surgery.

A South American doctor — Dr. Espinoza — performed the emergency surgery. I was given medication that caused me to drift off into a dream-like state. Just as I was beginning to relax, a searing stench awoke me with a start. A nightmare unfolded before me as this putrid, nauseating odor permeated the entire operating room. A deep sense of humiliation overwhelmed me . . . I silently wished to God I was dead.

I heard Dr. Espinoza yell, *"Oh, my God!"* He began pulling out what looked like large pieces of liver, about a foot long, from my vaginal canal. It was rotting placenta, remnant in my womb during delivery.

Dr. Espinoza demanded to know when my baby was born. When the nurse informed him that it was May 14th, he repeated several times in total disbelief, "TEN DAYS! I can't *believe* this!" Irately, he demanded to know the names of both doctors who had delivered my baby.

I was kept in the hospital overnight. When I awoke the following morning, it took every ounce of strength to lift my head one inch off the pillow. Dr. Espinoza informed me that it was a miracle that I was still alive. He explained to me that the decay from the rotting placenta could have entered my bloodstream at any time. If it had I would have died of toxic poisoning. The poison from the decay could have also entered my breast milk and killed my newborn. With that information I finally understood the gravity of what had been done to me.

Dr. Espinoza apologetically explained to me that he wished he could testify on my behalf but he was required as a stipulation of his employment to sign a document barring him from testifying against another physician regardless of the circumstances. He added that he was leaving to go back to his native country to practice medicine; the lack of ethics he witnessed in this country's medical profession prompted him to make this decision. I sadly realized, after what I had experienced, how badly we need more doctors like him in this country.

As I entered the hallway to leave the hospital that afternoon, I caught a glimpse of the White doctor standing in the hallway. When our eyes briefly met, he quickly looked away and almost ran in the opposite direction down the hallway. At that moment, I was absolutely certain that both doctors knew exactly in what condition they had sent me home, and the risks to my life and that of my newborn.

* *

Following this incident, I sank into deep periods of severe depression. I did contact a lawyer to investigate my experience. Upon his investigation, all charges were suddenly dropped for the emergency surgery where the decaying placenta was removed from my womb. However, I was finally told by my lawyer that because I and my infant did not die or suffer permanent physical damage, we simply did not have a case. What the lawyer failed to tell me was that this was not a civil case but a *criminal negligence* case and should have gone to court as such.

I paid the ultimate price: I was denied the joy of the most profound experience in a woman's life by the verbal insults, the medical incompetence, the unnecessary endangerment to my life and that of my infant, and the severe periods of depression I suffered due to the overwhelming humiliation I was forced to experience during the removal of the decaying placenta remnant in my womb. No one for the rest of my life can ever give back the moments that should have been mine to cherish rather than dread.

38

Is She With You?

The strong, glaring sun kept peeking into the crevices of the receiving blanket shielding my infant's eyes. As I struggled to keep her face hidden beneath a tiny patch of shade, I suddenly grew uncomfortable. I felt the hostile stare of three young White men who stood behind a counter distributing beer to the public.*

As my husband approached the counter and requested a cup of beer, one of the men pointed to me and casually asked, "Is she with you?"

Ramon looked over at me and smiled. "She is my wife."

One of the three men filled a paper cup with beer and started to hand it to my husband. As he reached out to take it, the young man holding the beer threw it in Ramon's face. All three men roared with laughter as the beer burned my husband's eyes and dislodged his contact lens. As he blindly stumbled back, I guided him to a nearby bench. His facial features were twisted with pain as

---

* This major theme park, upon being contacted, declined to make a statement defending or apologizing for the behavior of their employees.

he flung his head forward and pulled open each eye with his left hand, allowing his contact lens to fall into the palm of his right hand.

I could see my husband's hurt swelling up in his eyes like a little boy. However, his machismo would not allow him to cry, especially in public and in front of a woman . . . a White woman. It deeply pained me to realize that my white skin was going to be the whip on my husband's back. Our interracial marriage came with a very high price tag that would later prove too much for us to pay.

39

Sent Home to Die

I felt the wet morning dew touch my face as I hurriedly locked the front door of my apartment. I balanced my two-year-old daughter with one arm and my purse with the other as I scurried down a long row of cement steps. One of my sisters-in-law lived in an apartment at the foot of the hill.

As I opened the rickety screen door to her apartment, her six-week-old newborn was lying on the sofa. I normally would have dropped off my daughter and proceeded to go to work, but something deeply disturbed me. As I moved closer to my daughter's tiny cousin, I noticed a bluish tinge in the pigment of his skin. I gently pulled open the thin receiving blanket to examine him more closely. His breathing was labored and heavily congested. I knew that this baby was in trouble and needed to be in an oxygen tent.

In her broken English, my sister-in-law explained that the doctor gave her medicine for the baby and told her to keep him at home. In my broken Spanish, I explained that if we did not take him to County Hospital right away, he was going to die. I helped dress her three other small children for the bus ride.

154

＊＊

As we mounted the crowded bus with four small children and an extremely ill infant, frightening images of the past came back to haunt me: I saw my mother standing at the entrance of County Hospital as my baby brother stopped breathing; I felt my mother's panic as the nurse ripped my baby brother from her arms and ran down the corridor to place him in an oxygen tent. Now, as I looked at my sister-in-law's infant, the same panic encroached upon me. I tried to mask my feelings behind a show of composure and an air of confidence I did not really feel, to reassure my sister-in-law that everything was going to be all right. Deep down inside I knew differently.

When we finally arrived at County Hospital, it was like a busy meat counter where you take a number — regardless of the gravity of your illness. People lined the walls and filled the chairs in the overcrowded waiting room. Loud coughs sprayed through the air; children with visible measles and chicken pox covered with white paste played dangerously near pregnant mothers and newborn infants.

As one hour slipped by, I informed the receptionist that my sister-in-law's infant had pneumonia and needed to be placed in an oxygen tent; I was told we would have to wait our turn. As I examined the tiny infant, laboring harder with each breath, a hint of purple now mingled with the bluish tinge of his skin. I tried to remain calm because my sister-in-law never had a child with pneumonia and did not know the gravity of this illness.

When a second hour slipped by, we were finally called. We stood in a hallway — not an examination room. The young White doctor hurriedly peered into the receiving blanket and immediately wrote a prescription for more medication. This infant was having such difficulty breathing that I heard him while standing three feet away.

I am not really sure what happened next, but something snapped inside of me. The panic I experienced earlier was completely gone. I suddenly realized that this child's life had been placed in my hands. What I did within the next few moments would determine if another human being lived or died.

I turned to the doctor and stared directly at his name tag as I loudly warned, "If you don't put this baby in an oxygen tent right now and he dies, I will sue *you* and all of County Hospital!"

Like a wild dog measuring the strength of his adversary, the doctor searched my eyes for any hint of fear. He then ordered a nurse to place the infant in an oxygen tent and admit him as a patient. My sister-in-law looked at me; I motioned to hand the baby over to the nurse. Tears slowly streamed down her face as she began to understand the gravity of her son's illness.

My sister-in-law called her husband who joined us a short time later. They both sat there helplessly watching their tiny son frantically gasping for air. A nurse wandered into the room and announced that it was hard to say, given his extremely young age and condition, if he would survive. After waiting over two hours for *any* medical attention, and then getting a doctor who had to be threatened with a lawsuit before he would treat the pneumonia, I honestly felt as though I were standing in an insane asylum instead of a hospital. The irony overwhelmed me.

✶ ✶

I am very happy to announce that the infant *did* survive and is now a very handsome and healthy teenager. However, not all children are that lucky. Many are sent home to die because poverty begins at birth. There is no grace period that allows children to be sheltered from the brutal reality of poverty . . . a reality for which many children pay with their lives.

40

The Final Blow

My niece Marisa came rushing up the steep cement steps that led to my Highland Park apartment and breathlessly announced, "Aunt Kathy, your father's on the phone!"

I was too stunned to speak. My father had contacted my mother and requested my phone number; my mother had not notified me. I was completely unprepared to accept this phone call after waiting fourteen years for my father's return.

All of my childhood dreams — where my father would one day come back out of nowhere to rescue me with open arms — sped through my mind like an old movie that never loses its charm. The deep yearning that only my father could fulfill sparked an ember of hope that maybe *this time* I could make things different . . . I could make my father love me the way he once did.

Dazed, I dismounted the cement steps to my sister-in-law's apartment and slowly lifted the phone to my ear. "Hello?"

The instant I heard my father's voice, I felt emotionally transformed to the little girl he left behind. Following the unnatural formal introductions between a daughter and her father, I longed to curl up in his lap and hide like a child from my sixteen long years of loneliness.

In my mind, I had created a sacred place where I could secretly love my father, in spite of all the atrocities for which he was responsible. A curtain of silence had kept this place hidden in my heart. Now, that heavy curtain was about to be lifted; the final blow stood behind it.

Without a second thought, my father — the same man who condemned me to experience my childhood in the squalid conditions of the ghetto — now condemned me for having a baby at eighteen. I stood there in a complete state of shock, tightly clutching the phone. That sacred place inside of my soul died and for a moment I wanted to kill my father. I wanted to rip him to pieces with my bare hands so he could feel just a fraction of the horrendous pain he had inflicted upon me . . . I wanted *him* to feel what it was like to be emotionally butchered and left to die.

✶✶

I would like to conclude this chapter by saying that I have done a great deal of healing since I was twenty. I have been able through prayer and spiritual development to reach a place within myself where I no longer have a need to hate my father. Instead, I pity my father because he missed out on five precious children and seven beautiful grandchildren who would have filled his life with so much love.

41

To Serve and Protect

The whispering melody of crickets sang as a silvery, round moon playfully peeked through a black velvet sky. In awe of nature's majesty, Ramon and I sauntered hand in hand through the beauty of the night.

Our moment of bliss was suddenly interrupted when a police car pulled up right next to us. The White police officer, still sitting in his car, poked his head through the window and closely examined us before he casually asked, "Is she your whore?"

My husband remained completely still. In his hand, now tightly clutched around mine, I felt the silent scream of his rage buried deeply in his soul.

The beautiful night was transformed into a gripping chill that ripped through a bloodshot moon and overpowered the sweet cricket song. The gentle breezes were now cold winds slapping me in the face as I watched my husband crumble before me.

I helplessly stood there, thinking the danger to our lives had passed, when my eye caught a glimpse of a piece of metal inside the police car. I continued to focus my eyes on the object: the outline of a gun in the right hand of the officer transcended the darkness inside the police car. My deepest dread evolved at that moment . . . I realized that this police officer intended to kill us if my husband dared to say one word to defend the honor of his own wife.

My husband and I were rendered completely powerless. This policeman's omnipotence exceeded all authority as he held our lives in checkmate with his psychological chess game . . . nerves and raw emotion buried beneath a steep mountain of terror. While the jagged edges of fear threatened to unravel my calm exterior, I extinguished every inner feeling that emerged. There was no place for human feelings in a world where they cost you your life.

My husband was emasculated that day. This was the final blow. The ignorance . . . the racism . . . the violence . . . the unrelenting hate finally took its toll on both of us — leading up to the eventual dissolution of our marriage.

PART IX

The Internal Environment: Teaching Ghetto Children To Look Within

42

Psychology of the Mexican-American

College opened up many doors to me, but none of them quite so abruptly as two courses — Psychology of the Mexican-American 410A and 410B — at Cal State in Los Angeles. These courses lead me through doors that dramatically changed the way I perceived myself and the environment that shaped me during my childhood.

＊＊

As papers and pencils rustled in the background, a very young Hispanic college professor sauntered into our classroom. His eyes conveyed a sincere love for teaching; he effortlessly wove a natural sense of humor into the presentation of his lessons. He understood us better than we understood ourselves, but always tried to make us feel like we were his intellectual equals.

On many occasions, he shared his genuine feelings about different things. He felt free to be himself, and his freedom made me feel free to explore my own feelings.

I remember one lecture in particular. His eyes teared as he shared some very difficult personal feelings. He was lecturing about how education changes people and, in that process, sometimes others that we dearly love can no longer accept us because we are different. His Ph.D. had created a distance between him and some of the people he loved.

It was the first time I had ever witnessed, in a positive way, a college professor with enough courage to be honest with his feelings and therefore vulnerable with his students. He was teaching a tremendous truth ... about knowledge and the overwhelming power it holds to create permanent changes that make it impossible for us to return to an earlier and perhaps more comfortable stage in our development ... about changes that sometimes make others around us uncomfortable because we have entered the place that incites fear in most people: the unknown.

Slowly, and for the first time, my childhood began to make sense to me. The ghetto had imparted a knowledge and created a permanent, internal change that would live inside me for the rest of my life: how I looked at others and how I perceived myself. What was once a painful blur filled with shame and guilt became a clear picture of cause and effect. I was an innocent child caught between an emotionally disturbed father and a mother who chose to place me in the most dangerous environment in America: the ghetto.

Perhaps it was the grace of God that brought me to that college classroom where the truth opened my eyes. I learned to see that real blindness is not a physical handicap but a developmental one. My newly formed awareness gave me the courage to do something I would normally have never done: write about my childhood.

I wrote about one of my personal friendships. When the paper was returned, I was instructed to see my professor after class. As I ventured down the long hallway leading to his office, confidence to speak about my childhood wavered. I entered his office and he requested that I take a seat. He slightly tilted his head, leaned back in his chair, and warmly smiled. I tensed with anticipation. "Where did you grow up?"

I never imagined that such a simple question would be so difficult to answer. I instinctively knew that my answer would lead to many more questions that I was not emotionally prepared to answer. My eyes fell away as I whispered in a barely audible voice, "Los Angeles."

He pressed further. "*Where* in Los Angeles?" His smiled broadened as though he thought he was on the verge of ferreting out my little secret. He seemed to be able to look through me as he remarked, "You even walk like a Mexican woman."

Instantly I felt naked and frightened as I hurriedly gathered up my books and headed towards the door.

When I returned to his class the following week, I felt awkward and withdrawn, and sat at the back of the class near the door. I never found the courage to discuss his comment or what prompted him to make it. However, that comment opened a door in me that would have never been otherwise opened.

For the first time in my life, he made me *think* about the fact that growing up with Mexican and Black people had an impact on my development. I realized that I had been socialized in subtle ways in which I was not even aware .

* *

On the first day of the following semester, I walked into the classroom and found the instructor writing on the blackboard: *Psychology of the Mexican-American 410B.* His youth was buried in the deep facial grooves upon the coarse surface of his face. The professor's rough, swarthy hands echoed the hardships of the past. Strenuous physical labor built his sturdy body. Though his past experiences had prematurely erased his youth, his gentle eyes had not been touched by time.

I was strangely enamored, in a spiritual way, by this very quiet and deep man whose eyes seemed to convey more than his words. All of his lectures were heartfelt, but one in particular touched me the deepest.

It was a warm day and the slight breezes slipping through the classroom windows felt very refreshing. I remember our instructor's sweat-covered brow as he described a very troubled person in which he had taken an interest. He revealed that this person was suffering from acute alcoholism and spoke of this person's environment as completely lacking the encouragement and moral support necessary to help overcome his problems. I was stunned by his incredible insight into human behavior and deeply moved by the genuine compassion exhibited towards the pain of another human being.

At one point during this lecture, his eyes welled up as he painfully talked about the role ghetto parents unwittingly play in destroying their own children. I instantly thought about my mother and the many biting remarks that deeply cut me as a child. There had always been tremendous conflict between my mother and me; however, this was the first time I ever made a conscious connection between that conflict and my childhood development.

As I sat there, deeply in thought, his unexpected words rang out across the classroom and struck me right in the heart: *"If you lived in Aliso Village, you would be an alcoholic, too!"*

I was instantly jolted back to that tiny space in Aliso Village where I spent my childhood, dodging my mother's violent outbursts of rage caused by her alcoholism. Shrouded in shame, I walked through my childhood trying to hide my mother's pain. I battled as a flood of emotions now threatened to break through my calm exterior.

Instinctively, I wanted to race out of that classroom and far away from my life. Trapped in the center row and surrounded by my classmates, I hid deeply within myself a frightened girl and her alcoholic mother who had lived in Aliso Village.

Earlier, I had turned in a paper about my friendship with Angela. When it was returned, I noticed at the top of the paper, "See me after class." I slowly maneuvered my way through the crowds of students in the hallway and reluctantly passed through the threshold of my instructor's office doorway. With a look of bewilderment etched across his face, his eyes cautiously studied me for a moment before he spoke. His complete disbelief formed into a question. "How did you come by such intimate knowledge of the Mexican people?"

I became momentarily paralyzed, knowing that his direct question exacted an honest answer. Finally, I said in a soft whisper, "I grew up in Aliso Village."

Startled, he shouted, "You grew up in Aliso Village! How can that be?" Deeply upset, he rapidly paced back and forth in his office searching for something else to say. He made me feel as though I had invaded his private domain. Without any further conversation, I left his office. I completed the course and we never spoke about that day again.

**

I learned a great deal from both of these psychology classes. I discovered how perception is shaped by experiences. My instructor's perception did not include a White person growing up in Aliso Village.

I was no longer the middle-class White person shaped by the values, customs, beliefs, and experiences common to my own race ... that ended at six years of age. For eleven years following that, I was shaped by the values, customs, beliefs, and experiences of Mexican and Black ghetto children. As all children do, I internalized what I learned.

For years, I experienced a turmoil I did not understand. It was in these two Mexican-American psychology courses that I came to recognize the source of that turmoil: I was a psychological hybrid of two different worlds.

I had unwittingly inherited an in-depth perception of Mexican and Black cultures. I did not learn to look at these people with the preconceived notions and bias common to the adult mind — I had learned to see them through the eyes of a child.

43

Filling in the Blank Spaces

Unlike my childhood ghetto friends, I was always aware of the world outside the ghetto because of my exposure to it in the first six years of my life. In their perception, there *was* no world outside the ghetto.

In studying psychology and child development in college, I learned to recognize the significance of these early stages in a child's development and how a perception of self, others and the world is developed as a result.

Ghetto children, through no fault of their own, are forced to embrace an extremely hostile and perverse world which they internalize and accept as being a natural part of themselves. The internal problems begin with this process.

Young children do not possess the skill to discriminate; all things appear normal. In the case of ghetto children, this includes watching drug-infested breezeways, observing prostitution rings, witnessing random killings, often being ignored by social workers, experiencing many police that deride their parents and fail to protect and serve, and being subjected to numerous doctors that send children home to die.

I pull together these particular personal experiences to demonstrate the powerful negative forces that shape a young ghetto child's mind. In this process, a child emerges overwhelmed with sorrow and fear . . . fear of being ill or injured because you will be abandoned . . . fear of voicing your honest opinions because you might be killed . . . fear so entrenched that it often stunts the emotional and mental development of ghetto children. This is further compounded by ghetto school systems that are quick to slap the label "slow learner" over problems that they are unwilling to acknowledge and are unprepared to resolve.

Through the study of child development and psychology courses, ghetto children can begin to develop an understanding of their own maturation process, providing them with the tools to fill in the blank spaces of their own development. I highly recommend that child development and psychology courses be extended to ghetto children in junior high and high school, reaching all those who would otherwise not be exposed to these kinds of courses.

The complex web of gripping problems that entrap most ghetto children will begin to become less tangled when examined, not by professionals who have not experienced them, but by the children themselves. In the final analysis, ghetto children need to develop the inner tools provided by psychology courses. These inner tools will open their eyes to their own fears so they can walk beyond the psychological bars that imprison them.

44

The Ugly Duckling

As a student teacher, I was very excited and enthusiastic about becoming a fully certified teacher, and determined to be different than most I had experienced at Hollenbeck and Roosevelt. I was going to take a personal interest and assist my students in developing their individual potentials. I was going to make a difference in the world.

I had studied math methods courses in college on how to teach math concepts to children through the use of Cusinaire rods (small wooden rods that come in ten graduated sizes) with the theory that very young children could be taught abstract concepts through the use of concrete objects. I had a class of six year olds . . . a perfect opportunity to try out what I had learned. I was granted permission by my master teacher to use the rods.

I went to the school supplies room and searched for the Cusinaire rods. I discovered them high on a shelf inside plastic containers. A thick blanket of dust whirled down towards my face as I pulled each container from the shelf.

To my surprise, it seemed that the containers had never been opened. I wiped the dust off each container and took them to my classroom. I distributed one container to each student in the class and began the lesson. I was aware that they already knew addition and subtraction, so I announced that we would be learning how to do something new with numbers.

About thirty pairs of eyes carefully studied the unfamiliar word I printed in large block style on the blackboard: FRACTIONS. One child in the class did recognize the word and pointed out to me that fractions are not supposed to be taught in the first grade.

"How many of you like to pretend?"

All hands quickly shot up into the air. I explained that they were going to *pretend* that they were old enough to learn fractions that day. All eyes were glued to the blackboard. I had stimulated their curiosity and they were eager to proceed with the lesson.

I explained that each container in front of them held brightly painted wooden rods of ten different sizes and instructed them to spill out the contents on their desk. I had the students organize the wooden rods into ten groups according to size. I asked each student to select three rods from the third largest group and lay them down in a straight line.

"Take one rod from the straight line and tell me the number value of that rod."

"Three!" they all shouted.

"Put the rod back into the straight line and add the number value of each rod together. What is the number value of all three rods added together?"

"Nine!"

"Now, pick up one rod from the straight line. The rod you hold in your hand is one third of nine. Pick up a second rod. If one rod equals one third, then two rods equal how many thirds?"

Without hesitation, the entire class shouted, "Two thirds!"

On the blackboard I wrote "1/3 x 9 equals?" . . . the students shouted, "Three!"

I wrote "2/3 x 9 equals?" . . . the students shouted, "Six!"

I wrote "3/3 x 9 equals?" . . . the students shouted, "Nine!"

By the end of that afternoon, these six-year-olds who had never worked with fractions could multiply 1/2 x 2, 4, 6, 8; 1/3 x 6, 9, 12; 1/4 x 4, 8, 12; and 1/5 x 5, 10, 15 with complete comprehension.

Excitedly, I thought that what I had learned in math methods class works! You can teach a very young child abstract concepts through the use of concrete objects. I was sure the school would share my excitement.

I enthusiastically approached the administration office and was met with an attitude of indifference rather than enthusiasm. It was explained that, in order to incorporate such an idea into the curriculum, it would first have to be presented to the school board, voted upon and passed. The chances of it being passed would be very slim because of the administrative expense to incorporate a new teaching method, the cost of the additional materials needed and the additional training of teachers.

I felt deeply frustrated and disappointed. I believed that some-day when I became a fully certified teacher (instead of a student teacher) things would be different. I would teach my students to *comprehend* concepts instead of trying to *memorize* them. I believed that learning was not about memorization. Even a tiny mouse could be taught to memorize responses. Learning, in my opinion, was about exploring ideas and having a desire to understand *why*. Learning was a natural curiosity with which we are born to be nurtured and cherished all of our lives.

✳ ✳

With a formidable determination to become a teacher, I worked a swing shift as a payroll clerk from three in the afternoon until eleven in the evening, while I did my student teaching from eight in the morning until one in the afternoon. In addition, I contin-ued to raise my daughter as a single parent.

During my last year in college, my five-foot-seven-inch stature dropped from one hundred and twenty pounds to one hundred and five. I was beginning to suffer from fatigue but something inside would not let me give up.

A short time later, I became a credentialed teacher and was given a sixth grade class. I was so excited and proud to finally be able to call myself a teacher! I believed that *now* I would be allowed to make a difference in children's lives.

On my first day, all the new faces piled into the classroom to take their seats. It was a large class — over thirty students — and all were Mexican. Three had been identified by the school as slow learners. I decided that I really wanted to get to know my students as individuals.

I gave a lot of thought as to how I could accomplish this and came up with an idea: I glued a mirror inside of a shoe box. I asked each student to come up to the front of the class, look into the shoe box and write about the first thing they saw. When all of the students had finished coming up and had taken their seats again, one student inquired why I wanted him to write about himself.

"Even though test scores and learning levels are helpful," I explained, "many times they fail to tell the whole story or paint the entire picture. Maybe everyone in this class is reading, writing and doing math at the highest level of their ability. However, if just *one* of you in this class is not, it is my responsibility to recognize that and help you develop to the highest level of your abilities."

Instantly, more than thirty pencils busily scurried across the paper in front of them, pouring out their thoughts and feelings about everything. I took the papers home that night and spent the weekend carefully reading each one. They wrote about their families, friends, previous teachers and, most importantly, about *themselves*.

One paper stood out from all the rest. It was written by a student named Michelle — one of the three students that had been identified as a slow learner. She wrote in an upbeat and happy tone about her large family and friends. Then her paper became melancholy: "My teachers always think that I am not smart."

The other two slow learners performed consistently at a much lower level than the rest of the class. However, Michelle would always finish her work long before the other two, and read a book after she completed her work.

I set up a daily schedule that allowed me to spend a little extra time with her. I bought *The Ugly Duckling*, a story about overcoming feelings of inferiority told on a level which was perfect for a child to understand. We covered small parts of the story together every day. Slowly, I watched her self-confidence build; her reading performance showed weekly improvement.

In the midst of all this, Halloween arrived. The school was having a parade and my students were very excited about participating. Some expressed concern about not being able to afford costumes. I enthusiastically suggested that we all make Halloween costumes from cardboard boxes.

I instructed each student to bring in a large cardboard box that would fit comfortably around their bodies. The day before the parade, they transformed their boxes into radios, televisions, clocks, airplanes, buses, cars, bugs, birds and other animals. The end result was astonishing; their faces beamed with pride and I praised their creativity.

The following day, my students entered the classroom filled with excitement and anticipation about participating in the Halloween parade, and pride about their self-made costumes. As the parade commenced, all of my students eagerly marched out of the classroom to take their places. One little boy from another class was wearing an intricate, store-bought costume . . . he won first prize.

No recognition was given to *any* of the other children in the school for their costumes. My students returned to the class throwing their cardboard creations down on the floor and yelling, "These dumb boxes!"

I was infuriated at the school for their lack of sensitivity to these children's feelings and their lack of recognition for the elaborate creativity each one had demonstrated.

✳ ✳

My "special needs" student continued to improve; my work with her helped to take my mind off the Halloween incident.

During the Christmas season, her reading level finally rose to the rest of the class. I remember how her eyes lit up when I told her she could read as well as anyone else in the class. "*You* did this, Michelle. *You* accomplished this. I think you should go to college."

"College?" she responded in complete surprise.

"You know, Michelle, when I was a little girl I did not think I was smart enough to go to college either."

Her eyes widened. "You didn't?"

"Someone had to tell me I could do it before I believed that I could. But once I believed, no one could stop me." She pulled her head back slightly and just looked at me. "I made it through college and I am not any smarter than you are."

Suddenly her eyes gleamed with a pride that I had not seen before. She believed me and, for the first time in her life, she believed in herself. It was a beautiful sight to behold.

I thought the school would be pleased to learn that this student could now read at grade level and had been misidentified as a slow learner. However, when I made this fact known to the school, I was told that it was my job to teach and not to identify the learning level of students. If a child is identified as a slow learner, I am to accept that without question and not attempt to change it.

I was stunned and returned to my classroom deeply depressed. For several days I gave the entire situation a great deal of thought. I had helped a little girl learn to believe in herself which greatly improved her ability to learn. Several times I asked myself: *is not what I did for this child the essence of what it means to be a teacher?*

I thought back to my childhood friend Angela. I realized that both Angela and Michelle just needed a teacher who was willing to look beyond the surface and stimulate their dormant potential. Unfortunately, Angela never found that quality in a teacher; I clearly remembered what it did to her.

I had to make a choice between what I believed was right and my job; I decided to give up teaching and never return. I knew I could never sit in a classroom and allow a child's potential to die.

On my last day, a small group of girls in the class presented me with a gift. I was deeply touched as I pulled the delicate gold charm from the tiny square box. The charm was shaped into a sun with two eyes and a broad smile that perforated the center. I was overwhelmed by the thought and expense that these little girls went through just to give me this gift. I told them that I would always cherish it.

I walked over to Michelle and explained that the school administrators were like the ducks in *The Ugly Duckling* — they did not recognize what she could do. I reminded her to always remember what she had learned from the story and someday she would prove that all of those people were wrong.

She handed me a gift — a 5x7 picture of a peaceful, soft blue lake at the foot of a lush, green mountain covered with trees. The picture was inside a wooden frame with a glass top. A black silhouette of a duck flying freely towards a marsh was imprinted on the surface of the clear glass. In the upper left-hand corner, above the mountains and across the soft, blue sky, the words "Everyday is special to those who love beauty" were printed.

As I turned to walk out of the classroom for the last time and glanced down at the gift in my hand, I realized that children give back to us what we give to them.

Epilogue

It is my firm belief that it is difficult to develop compassion until we learn to see, with our hearts as well as our minds, another person's pain. In writing this book, I have attempted to provide you with the most intimate details of my childhood and that of others, so that you could examine the complex problems and the overwhelming gravity of the forces that systematically tear ghetto children down.

I always knew that I saw the world differently than my ghetto friends. My first six years outside the ghetto helped me develop a perception of the world that extended beyond the ghetto. My ghetto friends, all of who were born in the ghetto, never had the opportunity to see the world *outside* the ghetto.

In their perception, the ghetto was the entire world; in my perception, it was only a part of the world. I believe that this was the main reason I could walk beyond the psychological boundaries that entrap most ghetto children.

This book can be used as a teaching tool:

◆ Teachers could be taught how to see beneath the surface of ghetto children and stimulate their dormant potential.

◆ Doctors could be taught to see the awesome responsibility that is placed in their hands and the long-term impact their behavior has on ghettos.

◆ Social workers could be taught to see the powerful role they might play in protecting and nurturing children.

◆ Policemen could be taught to see that the greater power is not in their wooden clubs and loaded guns, but in their willingness to treat ghetto people with the same dignity and respect that all people deserve.

◆ The general public could be taught to see ghetto children from where a ghetto child lives — collectively changing the perception held of ghetto children throughout this nation.

◆ Ghetto children could be taught to see their own development . . . to see the psychological boundaries created by their experiences . . . to feel the freedom that only real knowledge can bring. When we offer this, they can develop the tools within themselves and escape the ghetto.

Home

Should I lace the skies with butterflies
All standing in a row
Or touch the springs with silver wings
And home my heart will flow
Should I spread the stars so very far
To touch my heart's desire
Or kiss the moments in my hand
And guard them with a fire
Should I comb the waves that sorrow paves
With a golden comb
Or span the soft blue heavens
Where my heart can find its home.

– Kathleen Bishop

Dedicated in loving memory of
Edward Romero, Jr.
1975 – 1992